Whose Kids
Are These Anyway?

True Confessions of a Family Man

Whose Kids
Are These Anyway?

True Confessions of a Family Man

KEN SWARNER

A Perigee Book

13952452

A Perigee Book
Published by The Berkley Publishing Group
A division of Penguin Group (USA) Inc.
375 Hudson Street
New York, New York 10014

Copyright © 2003 by Ken Swarner
Text design by Tiffany Kukec
Cover design and illustration by Larry Martin

First edition: May 2003

Library of Congress Cataloging-in-Publication Data
Swarner, Ken.
Whose kids are these anyway? / Ken Swarner.—1st Perigee ed.
p. cm.
ISBN 0-399-52881-4 (pbk.)
1. Parenting—Humor.   2. Parent and child—Humor.   I. Title.

PN6231.P2 S93 2003
814'.6—dc21   2002035504

Printed in the United States of America

10 9 8 7 6 5 4 3 2 1

Contents

Judgment Day

> "Grown-ups never understand anything for themselves, and it is tiresome for children to be always and forever explaining things to them."
>
> —Antoine de Saint-Exupery

I have been a parent for several years, and I am absolutely stuffed with all the words I have had to eat.

Before my wife and I had children, one of the games we'd play was Pin the Verdict on the Child. We'd take an occasion where a child runs up and down the aisle of a wedding, doesn't say thank you when given a gift, or wears ratty clothes at a formal function, and then we'd discuss in detail why that's bad and how we wouldn't allow our future kids to do that.

I loved that game. It was fun to play. I had no idea how ugly payback would be.

Frankly, there's been nothing more unsettling than having a child of my own enter this world to publicly manifest, at one time or another, most of the abhorrent traits I once denounced in other kids.

For all the times I remarked about the poor behavior of someone else's child, mine have knocked food off grocery store shelves, thrown rocks at dogs, and forgotten to say thank you to relatives.

Because I once pointed out another child's poor eating habits in public, I've had to watch in horror while my kids chewed up their bread rolls in a posh restaurant and pretended to barf on their salad plates.

Just the other day, the class pictures came back with my son's tongue sticking out . . . which wouldn't have been nearly so bad if he hadn't also left the house wearing his ripped "Barney's a Mama's Boy" T-shirt.

In addition to eating my words, I have also had to back-pedal on several policy statements I made before my children were born.

My first retraction was allowing the children to sleep in my bed. Some people worry that the "family bed" creates over-dependency, disturbed sleep patterns, and bad habits. I used to tell everyone the same thing. But when I realized it would take 1,378 consecutive nights of ushering my kids back to their rooms before they'd give up trying to get in my bed, I raised the white flag and went back to sleep.

Once I reversed on that point, I opened the floodgates and have rescinded almost everything else I stood against before becoming a dad. I have allowed my kids to eat massive amounts of sugar, see PG movies, stay up late, and have dessert without finishing their vegetables.

I figure at this rate, my kids will be drinking before they're ten.

"Thanks for the martini, Dad."

"Sure, I hope it's not too dry."

Don't get me wrong, I have tried to live up to the expectations I placed on other parents. I even went five years without spanking before I finally broke down and reddened some little backsides.

It's getting to the point where I can't say anything without it biting me back later. I'm afraid to open my mouth.

I did, however, crack under the pressure the other day and told my daughter she couldn't date until she's sixteen.

"Na-uh," she said. "When I'm twelve."

Boy, that's going to be hard to swallow.

Of course, I can't help but think my experiences as a parent could translate to an effective birth control program for today's teenagers. All we need to do is bring various high school health classes around to my house and let them see the effects of having children. Quite frankly, I think it'll scare the crap out of most of them. They probably wouldn't consider having sex again for years . . . I know it's had that effect on my wife and me.

If that doesn't work, we can show them a home video of the time I was knocked out with the flu with a toddler at home.

Teacher: "And in this next scene, boys and girls, notice how the father is vomiting into the toilet while his little girl is pushing her Barbie car up and down his back."

Whose kids are these anyway?

1

My Rookie Year

"The beginning is the most important part of the work."

—Plato

When my wife went back to work after the birth of our first child, we had agreed that continuing him on breast milk would be ideal.

We went to the store and bought the deluxe breast pump. We purchased insulator bags for the bottles. We cleared out extra space in the refrigerator.

Six hours into the first day, my wife called me at work.

"Ken, I can't bear it anymore."

"Your job?" I asked.

"No, this breast pump," she complained. "I feel like a cow in the big city."

"In the city?"

"Well, actually in the toilet stall, where I just sat milking away my entire lunch break while listening to the young secretaries gossip over the noise of the hand blower."

"You sit on the toilet?"

"Well, where did you think I would do it?" she asked. "In the copier room? What would I say? 'Come on in guys—don't mind me, I'm just sucking nourishment from my breast. Oh, and by the way, the legal-size paper is over there on the table, under my blouse.'"

That night we regrouped. We reminded ourselves of the health benefits of breast milk, and my wife reconfirmed her desire to put her best foot forward.

She called me at noon the next day.

"I feel like I'm doing something illegal," she announced.

"Why?"

"Because I hide out in the bathroom."

"People don't care," I said. "I'm sure everyone supports your decision."

"Do you think so? What do you suppose people who don't know what I am doing in there think when they walk into the bathroom and all they hear is the low hum of an electrical device behind a bathroom stall?"

"Maybe your boss should provide a breast pumping room," I suggested. "Where the new mothers can . . ."

"Sit around watching each other pump their bare breasts?" she interrupted.

"Well . . ."

"Maybe we could also share home remedies for chapped nipples," she added sarcastically. "We could even take turns bringing snacks."

On the second night, we held hands and prayed. Still, my wife assured me, she was dedicated to breast milk.

Come the third day, she was on the phone by 10 A.M.

"There is only one stall close to the outlet to plug in my pump," she explained frantically.

"So?"

"So, I had to wait until the stall was free—which wasn't easy when my breasts were so engorged they began erupting—I had to open my bra and empty out on the floor."

"That's embarrassing," I said.

"Actually, the bad part is when the milk ran down around the feet of whoever was on the other side of the stall. I imagine she'll throw away her shoes after something like that."

When I got home, I noticed the deluxe breast pump and insulator bags were stuffed into the trash can.

I never said a word.

Just about everybody says a baby won't change their lives BEFORE the baby arrives. We tell that to our friends who worry we'll no longer see each other. We tell our boss who worries our production will fall. We even say it to the dog . . . but, quite frankly, babies tend to occupy a parent's every waking moment—which is weird considering they don't REALLY do anything. Even vacations change for new parents. You're all excited to take the baby on her first extended trip, you make reservations at a favorite restaurant, you're ready to eat, but then you can't because the baby is fussy. On the next day, you're excited for a swim in the resort's expansive pool with the swim-up bar, you switch into your floral swimsuit, but your spouse breaks the bad news: The baby is gassy. Even when the maids show up to clean the room, they have to wait in the hallway because the baby is pukey.

It's amazing you even had time to buy a souvenir considering the baby's diaper rash had you pinned down for six days.

Babies aren't just physically demanding—they tend to stretch the mental capacities as well. Personally, I find myself staring into space frequently trying to figure out the answers to dilemmas like the following:

An empty diaper bag: If you reach into the diaper bag in the morning, and all that's there is a Zwieback with a bite missing from it, what is the right answer to the following problem: If a baby travels without a diaper from point A (your home) to point B (the grocery store), what will keep the car seat drier? A. The old diaper, B. a dishtowel, or C. my wife's pajama bottoms.

The baby car seat: Man has long struggled with how to put in a car seat without requiring major medical attention. Exactly how do you lace the seat belt through the narrow holes in the back without either shredding the skin on your hand against the rough plastic or getting your hand stuck in there altogether while cars pass by your driveway wondering who's legs are flapping outside the car door?

The poop-free zone: Why is it that no matter when I change my child's diaper in the morning, she will do a doodle precisely at the moment I walk into the day care to hand her over to the staff? I could whip a new diaper on her in the backseat of my car while in the center's parking lot, and two seconds later, she'll number two. Also, why is it that the day care worker will take up my daughter, sniff the air, and say, "Oh, did we forget to change us this morning?" In these instances, is it acceptable to look at this person and reply, "Oh, did you do a doodle, too?"

Of course, the greatest challenge for new fathers is asking a male boss for paternity leave.

When I asked mine for four weeks leave, he looked at me as if I had just asked him for his pancreas.

My boss is from the old school. To say that he doesn't understand the new generation of fathers would be an understatement.

"Why do you want to do that?" he replied, getting a painful, bloated look on his face.

"I want to be home to hold my baby so he can smell me and feel comforted by my voice," I answered.

"Can't your wife do that?"

"What? Smell like me?"

I was the first one in our office to ask for such a thing. I am sure my boss had heard of paternity leave, but I suspect he thought it was something only people in Los Angeles or Europe did.

He shifted uncomfortably in his chair. "Why don't you just take an extra 30-minute lunch, drive home, and get smelled then?"

"I don't go home for lunch," I answered. "Besides, by the time I got there, I'd have enough time to kiss the baby and then leave."

He smiled hopefully. "At least that's something."

"That's true," I said. "Maybe I could just fax my love home. The baby could watch the paper come out of the machine while my wife says: 'Look, here come Daddy's words. Aren't they pretty? And wow, on company letterhead—he must really love you.'"

Regardless of how he felt, my boss granted the leave nonetheless. And when my son was born, I really enjoyed the time off with him.

What I didn't expect, however, was my boss calling me every couple days to discuss business.

"Ken, I need you to call over to our head office," he said on the phone one day. "They have a few questions only you can answer. In fact, if at all possible, maybe you could go there for just a short visit."

I told him I would try. But, later, I found out my wife had a doctor's appointment so I decided work would just have to get along without me.

The next day, my boss called again. "Did you get over there?"

"I tried, but my wife had an appointment."

"And?"

"And my son wouldn't fit in my briefcase."

"So, you're still planning to be out another two weeks?" he inquired.

"Yes."

"Tell me again, why is this so important?"

"Because," I said, "I don't want my little boy's first words to be 'Daddy' as he points to the postman."

He paused for a moment. "So what do you do all day? Doesn't the baby just sleep?"

"That, and I change his diapers, give him baths, and I do the 2 A.M. feeding."

"Aren't you doing that . . . that . . . ?"

"Breast-feeding thing?" I asked. "Yes, but we are switching off between that and breast milk we've stored in bottles."

"You're doing the bottle?"

"No, I'm breast-feeding," I exclaimed. "Which is okay, but boy, my nipples will be happier when my son can take a sippy cup."

There was silence on the other end for a few seconds, then, in a quiet voice, he said, "Gosh, I didn't realize guys did that now."

In a way, I feel sorry that my boss didn't understand what I was talking about. Of course, I am pretty sure he thought the same about me.

Nonetheless, I did spare my boss the gruesome details of one of parenting's greatest nightmares: baby spit-up.

I don't get it. You'd think babies would want to hold down their food. Is this God's plan? For a Supreme Being who invented some of the most complex and efficient systems in our universe, it's disconcerting to think that he purposely created a process where a hungry baby regurgitates a bottle shortly after finishing it, only to be hungry a few minutes later. (The only other known species to do this is college students, but they tend to deserve it.)

The spit-up phase seems to last an eternity. For a long time, my co-workers thought I lived near the beach because I frequently showed up to work with a milky-white patch on my shoulder, or (my favorite), the long, white stream cascading down my back.

"Seagull, Ken?"

"No," I'd answer. "Spit-up."

"Yours?"

The more parents I talk to, however, the more I've learned I'm not alone. Baby spit-up is a national epidemic. And what's especially frightening about this is that parents are never tagged while wearing a ratty T-shirt or garden clothes. A baby doesn't strike until the person holding him is wearing their Sunday best, miles away from a place to change.

That's why, on any given day, you'll see a handful of parents walking around looking like a fishing pier.

In fact, baby spit-up is so common, I'm surprised the nation's toy makers haven't jumped on the bandwagon and invented a Puking Patty doll we could give to our daughters.

"Look honey, I bought you a Puking Patty. See, you just press Patty's palm and she hurls on you."

Of course, what would happen if we all acted like that?

"Honey, that was great pot roast . . . *(ack)* . . . of course, I just wanted half of it."

To make matters worse, the major spit-up months center on a period when some babies are drinking formula. For those who can't remember this recycled smell because they lost their olfactory sense during that stage, let me remind you: The smell is like being trapped in an ammonia factory while your nostril hairs are on fire.

Formula spit-up is the worst smell on earth. (On a positive note, however, during the first few months when my newborn children were awake in the middle of the night, I'd use the spit-up on my clothes like smelling salts to ward off the sleep deprivation.)

All I can figure out is that this must be the ultimate baby joke. I am sure they get a big kick out of it when they spew all over us. I've noticed that when two babies are next to each other, they tend to smile and babble between themselves. Now I know what they're saying:

Baby 1: "Guess what?"

Baby 2: "What?"

Baby 1: "I vomited formula on my mommy's penny loafers this morning."

Baby 2: "Oooo—bad vomit?"

Baby 1: "Well, let's just say that when I'm older, I'm not playing dress-up with those shoes."

Of course, baby spit-up is only one of a billion things to know about parenting. As a public service, I'll let you in on some other information I have garnered. In fact, after careful research, I've developed a foolproof list of recommendations for new parents that will help you assimilate back into society after the birth of your child. (These tips and warnings have been tested in my home laboratory.)

1. Circumcision is NOT a lunch topic.

2. The likelihood of a child vomiting on you in the morning is directly related to the number of clean clothes you have hanging in your closet.

3. Always check to see if your socks match.

4. There is a Take Your Daughter to Work Day, but not a Take Your Newborn to Work Day.

5. Tie your shoes, keys, and wallet permanently to your body. This will save you thirty minutes every morning.

6. Pray that as you are rushing out the door, your spouse doesn't say, "Honey, come here . . . and bring the rectal thermometer."

7. Check under your nails for doo-doo.

8. Getting anywhere on time is overrated.

9. Keep lots of pictures of your cute new baby on your desk at work. (It's a lot harder to find someone with the guts to fire you.)

10. Develop a thick skin at work when the single employees stare at you when you're the last to arrive and the first to go home. Don't try to explain why you have to leave in the middle of a perfectly good workday to tend to a sick child.

11. Don't take your kids out on your work.

12. If you stay home to rest, you'll most likely spend the entire time trying to get things done.

13. Every once in a while, show off to your boss and stay a couple extra minutes past closing time.

14. When you announce to your spouse that you have to go away on business and you're really sorry she

is stuck at home with all of the midnight feedings, try not to smile or get caught high-fiving the dog.

15. Nothing breaks up a discussion faster than someone talking about her child's "irritable bowel syndrome."

I hope this helps!

2

Boy, Oh Boy!

"Boys will be boys."
—Anthony Hope

Letters from a dad to his teenage son:

MONDAY:
Son,
Good morning, unless of course you slept past noon, again.
While I am at work, please mow the lawn and put the grass
clippings in the recycle bin (not under the house).
Afterward, please walk your sister down to Lisa Rangale's
home. If Mrs. Rangale speaks to you, please don't grunt.
Try using some of that English language you learned at
school. How's the job-hunting going? Is it tough finding
summer employment a week before school starts?
Love,
Dad

P.S. Did I adopt your friends and not know it? One of them
asked me for $10 the other day, and another wanted to
know when Grandma was visiting. Then there's the kid

who's been on the couch for six weeks with the remote control in his hands. He's wearing my pajamas.

TUESDAY:
Son,
Good afternoon. The guest bathroom is for guests. You are
not a guest—even though you act like one. Were we invaded
yesterday by a band of pirates? There's not a lick of food in
the house—even the baking soda is gone. Guard the Jell-O
with your life.
Love,
Dad

P.S. Are those your initials mowed into the lawn?

WEDNESDAY:
Son,
Good afternoon. If you are going to kiss your girlfriend,
please have the courtesy to do it inside, rather than in front
of the mailboxes blocking Mrs. McCurdy next door from
getting her mail. She's 72 and was grossed out. You're not
too old for summer camp, you know.
Love,
Dad

P.S. I noticed you and your friends all bleached your hair
yesterday. Whose idea was it to do the same to the cat? She's
fixed and de-clawed—isn't that enough?

THURSDAY:
Son,
Good afternoon. Is that our toilet paper hanging in Mrs.

McCurdy's trees? I recognized our light blue two-ply. I'm not sure what music you were listening to in your room last night, but, before you bite off the head a bat or something, I think we should talk. Any idea when you might finish mowing the lawn?

Love,

Dad

P.S. I hope you have a nice day at home. I'm thinking about licensing our place as a youth hostel. Tell your friends I'll give them a special rate if they take their feet off the coffee table.

FRIDAY:

Son,

Good afternoon. The garage sale was an interesting and ingenious idea to compensate for your summer unemployment. However, I wish you had mowed the lawn before you sold my lawn mower. What's your position on military academies?

Love,

Dad

P.S. Someone's mom called this morning looking for her son. I asked her to describe the boy, but she couldn't remember what he looked like anymore (wait till she sees the hair). Anyway, she's coming over tonight to watch you kids eat— she's looking for the one who chews with his mouth open (I hope he has some other distinguishing mark). I pray it's not your friend who helped me push my car to the gas station this morning after you boys ran it dry last night. He bought me a doughnut and called me sir. I'd miss him terribly.

More than anything—household plumbing, cranky employers, or foot fungus—a son presents a man the most challenge. Especially mine. My son is bright, handsome, athletic, funny, everything a dad could want—but I see right through this.

I think my son is actually an alien placed on this planet to drive me NUTS.

For starters, if anyone reading this book is planning to be on Interstate 95 this summer, and you see a poor guy's sanity lying there, please let me know . . . it's mine.

I lost it somewhere between Reno and Las Vegas when my son said, "I think my shoe flew out the window."

"What do you mean, your shoe flew out the window?!" I asked, unable to see the road behind me through the rearview mirror because a huge stack of camping gear blocked the back window. "Didn't your mother tell you to keep that window closed?!"

"I had to throw out my peach pit," he explained.

"Your mom told you not to do that."

"It was sticky."

"Your sister managed to keep her pit inside," I pointed out.

"Yeah—she stuck it to the ceiling."

"It's a Christmas decoration," my daughter announced.

"Which shoe was it?" I asked.

"My high-tops."

"Your Desert Storm Action shoes?"

"Uh-huh."

My shoulders sagged. "So how did the shoe fall out?!"

"I don't know—my window was up," he assured me.

"Before or after the shoe fell out?"

"Before," he explained. "Maybe God did it."

My daughter made a "I know" sound through her lips:

"God probably did it because he kicked me this morning with that shoe."

"That wasn't my fault."

My wife had been staring at me throughout this conversation, so finally I had to ask, "What?"

"Aren't you turning around?" she asked.

"Around where?"

"Back to look for the shoe?"

"Yeah, right," I scoffed. "We're going to find a shoe that not only is designed to be camouflaged in a desert, but also has been called by God and is, right this moment, finding holy reconciliation in the desert?"

"That shoe cost $45," my wife explained. "I worked overtime to buy that."

Arguing about money with my wife is a lost cause. We went back. We searched fruitlessly for 30 minutes until I had a third-degree sunburn on my bald spot. Back on the road, it was dead silent in the car. I assumed everyone was reflecting on the events of the previous hour.

Finally, my son said, "I found my shoe."

"That's not funny," I exclaimed.

"No, really, it was under my seat—I guess it didn't fall out of the car after all. And look! My peach pit is inside it, too."

Sanity is a funny thing. Once you've lost it, it's very difficult to get it back.

Speaking of vacations, this year, the Swarners' annual summer car trip took us past Smokey the Bear's national museum and final resting place in Capitan, New Mexico.

We watched a half-hour documentary of the bear's life and death. We walked through the museum. We stopped by his grave site to pay our respects.

As we were leaving, my daughter faked a few tears as she

lamented melodramatically on the famous bear's demise—to which my son, stirring himself into reality, asked, "Smokey's dead?"

How did he miss that?

I used to think I wasn't communicating effectively with my boy, but I've come to learn that he is only a part-timer here on Earth. The rest of the time his mind is elsewhere—maybe on Pluto.

"Pluto's cold?"

Do you have a child like this? The son who sits in the room listening as you make dinner plans and afterward, replies, "So, what's for dinner?"

The son who runs in the house to fetch you a flashlight and a half-hour later you find him on the couch watching TV?

The son who has a major book report due the next day but can't remember where he last saw his book . . . let alone that he had a book report to do in the first place?

The son who, by all academic measurements, is fully capable and normal, yet accidentally takes his socks in the shower and then continues wearing them the rest of the day?

"My shoes are making a squishing sound."

We've tried many different ways to parent a child like this.

When my son was a toddler, we tied one of those doggie-leash-like things to his wrist so he wouldn't absentmindedly wander off in the mall. We stopped when he started barking.

When his teacher called to say our son wasn't doing his homework, we removed all the toys and distractions from his room so he'd concentrate on his assignments. Instead, he lost track of time pretending his socks were hand grenades and tossing them out the window at his little sister, the paperboy, and our neighbor's chow (who growled at the sock and then peed on it).

When he forgot to take his lunch to school for the tenth time in a year, we didn't bring it to him so he'd learn a valuable, albeit hungry lesson. Of course it backfired when the school principal gave him half of her lunch and sent a note home asking if we needed financial assistance.

Finally, we gave up and decided to allow nature to take its course—we chose to accept our son for who he was—no matter how many times we had to turn the car around and go home because he forgot his shoes.

Of course, we have to bite our tongues, like the time when my wife was scolding our daughter at the dinner table for constantly changing her clothes during the day.

"You only need to change your underwear once a day," she informed our little girl.

Suddenly, my son's face snapped to attention as if he just landed back on Earth after a long absence. "EVERY DAY?!" he exclaimed. "You never told me that!"

I wonder if his parents on Pluto have the same trouble?

I also wonder how his Pluto folks would answer this question: If you could have A., a smart, popular, good-looking, naturally talented, freeloading son who shared your life for all eternity and never left his studio apartment upstairs in your house, or B., a son who moved far away but was employed, which would you choose?

If you answered A, you're probably a strong candidate for a pet, and someone who should volunteer serving refreshments at a punk rock concert for needed shock therapy.

If you answered B, you're a red-blooded American parent who already has your five-year-old's college dorm picked out and a moving company on standby.

From the moment our children are born, we start grilling

them on the basics. What is your name? Why did you hit your sister? What do you want to be when you grow up?

This last question is the most important. After 20 years of communal living, parents aren't interested in excuses about the high cost of living or scaled-down workforces. They just want the kids to get out and send pictures of the grandchildren.

"What do you want to be when you grow up?" is as common a phrase in American homes as "I'll give you something to cry about!"

My son, however, is an exception to the rule. He has aspirations of employment, but he'll still be living with me when my Social Security check bounces. He wants to be an artist.

"A cutting artist," he says with a toothy grin.

The kid next door was born with a silver spoon in his mouth. My son came into this world with scissors.

In fact, when he popped out of the womb, he cut his own umbilical cord.

Let me explain. A cutting artist takes magazines, newspapers, dishtowels, cardboard, and airline tickets; cuts them out in odd shapes, then pastes, glues, tapes, tacks, or licks them on paper, walls, cousins, wood, or Mom's side of the bed.

Now, here's the best part: "They're free," my son explains. "I wouldn't want to charge for them."

"Oh, isn't that cute," my mom exclaimed, clutching her own Alasdair Swarner original titled "Jell-O Ad on Escrow Papers."

I scowled at her. "Do you have some nonprofit artists foundation or trust fund I don't know about? No? Then don't encourage the child!"

Frank down the street is a lucky dad. His son wants to be a brain surgeon. Joe at my office is raising a future shortstop for the Seattle Mariners. Their homes will be calm and orderly in fourteen years.

My son's masterpiece, "Phone Bill Caulked on Pillowcase," will be hanging in the Louvre, but he'll still be living with me when he's forty, chewing his food with his mouth open and forgetting to flush the toilet.

I'll probably be kicked out of Rotary for bringing one more starving artist into the world. I want to answer B to the above question, but sadly I must settle for C. Smart, good-looking, talented son who moves far away from home but returns four years later with 275 reams of paper, a gallon of rubber cement, and his college diploma nailed to the sole of his shoe.

Like I said, my son is a challenge. What's different about him from myself when I was a child, however, is that when I was a kid, one of the worst punishments my dad would conjure up was a week-long banishment to my room. No friends, no TV, no fresh air—from the moment I returned home from school until bedtime, just solitude. The weekend was especially agonizing.

Borrowing this tradition, I exiled my own son to his room recently when his fourth-grade report card indicated four missing assignments and a couple of disparaging remarks from his teacher. I wanted him to have time alone to assess his priorities.

When I arrived home the next evening, I asked my wife for a status report. I had assumed she'd declare that our son announced he had given his behavior serious thought, and he was now ready to plea-bargain his way out of jail.

Instead, I was told the only sound he had made thus far was a squeal of joy when he found his long-lost GI Joe buried under his mattress.

"Apparently," my wife explained, "he's rediscovered half his toys."

I was puzzled. Throughout that first evening, there were no tears or complaining coming from his room—except, of course, when he poked his head out and asked us to turn down the volume on the TV because he was trying to learn tai chi from a *Boy's Life* magazine.

As I went to bed, I dismissed these events as beginner's luck—after all, anyone can survive one day in his room. The next day would be different.

It was. In fact, I was told my son hadn't made a noise since he came home from school. As I stood outside his door, I admit that I couldn't help but smirk a little. I had imagined a very sorry little boy lying facedown on his bed, pledging he would do his homework from here on out. And, as I opened the door, I even expected some begging. Instead, he was hunched over his desk with a magnifying glass, arranging dead flies he found in his overhead light. He was going to press them in a scrapbook for his grandma and wanted to know if I would volunteer to sit on them.

What could I do? I removed all his playthings from his room and instructed him to think long and hard about his studies.

An hour later, I peeked in on him. He was sitting on his bed, staring into space. Another hour passed, and he was in his closet with his feet sticking out.

Finally I felt he was giving earnest thought to his responsibilities . . . until another hour later I caught him with two pebbles he found lodged in the tread of his shoes. He had named them Ivan and Ian, and as I walked into his room, he was firing them out of his mouth like cannonballs. He told me there was also an Igor, but he accidentally swallowed that pebble when Ivan ricocheted off the wall and hit him in the face.

I took the rocks.

Despite the setbacks, when I arrived home the next day, I

still expected to see a change of heart in my son. No child, I thought, could withstand THIS MUCH time alone in his room without anything to do.

"How's the little prisoner doing?" I asked my wife as I put down my briefcase.

"Well, the last time I looked," she said, "he was stringing his underwear together."

"As a means to escape out his window?"

"No—to make a hammock."

I gave up. Does anyone know how to put an imagination in time-out?

Better yet, maybe you have some advice for how I could have handled things when my son exclaimed "Guess what I have?" as he walked out of Sunday School.

"Let me guess," I replied. "You made rosaries with dried peas and string again?"

"Nope, this," he answered, bringing his hands around to show me.

"It's an empty sheet of paper," I said.

"Actually," he said with a big grin, "it's my homework. We're supposed to write a story about how our family talks about God together."

I couldn't believe this was happening. As a family, we were so busy rushing kids off to school, getting to work on time, volunteering for Cub Scouts and PTA, and watching soccer games on the weekends, that there has been little time for formal religious education at home. We could barely organize all four food groups into dinner. So, imagine my shock when suddenly, on a sunny Sunday, without warning, my son was poised to document our religious failings to his entire class?

"Yeah, the teacher wants us to write a hundred words about it," he continued.

Panicked, I silently prayed the dog would eat his homework.

"You know what I'm going to call my essay?" he asked.

"'My Parents Are Heathens'?"

"No. 'God Car.'"

I was mortified. "Because you think we won't let God into our house? That he has to sit outside in the garage? That we are on the Highway to Hell?"

"No." He laughed. "Because we talk about God when we are in the car. Remember Friday, on the way to the store, when you said God sees everything?"

"That's because you threw your sister's homework out the window."

"So?"

"So, I think your teacher is talking about prayer," I explained.

"We prayed in the car."

"When?"

"When you ran out of gas on the freeway."

"We asked God for a tow truck," I said.

"My teacher says you can pray for a lot of things."

"Is that what you are going to write about?"

"Uh-huh," he answered. "And about the time Claire nailed that mouse to the wood."

It's true. My daughter found a dead mouse in our backyard and instead of "not touching it" like I warned, she took a hammer and nailed the poor thing to a two-by-four.

She told me she did this as I was driving her and her brother to school.

Gathering up the courage, I asked, "Sweetie, why did you hammer a mouse to some wood?"

"Jesus was nailed to a cross," my darling child explained.

I shook my head. "That's true, sweetheart, but we don't use his sacrifice as a convenient excuse to pound holes into a dead rodent. We should respect our fellow creatures even when they have the bad timing to die in the shadows of a little girl armed with penny nails."

That explanation opened up a twenty-minute discussion about God and death while we cruised down the highway—a blip in a seemingly normal and hectic day, yet, as pointed out by my son, a "real-life" family moment. And considering we eat meals, dress, and make phone calls from our car, why not, I thought, have God along for the drive as well?

"See, we do talk about God," my son exclaimed.

I smiled, relieved he had something to write about.

"And how about when you said police are like our morals," he continued.

"Yep, I get the point now," I said.

"So why did your morals give you a speeding ticket . . . and why can't I tell Mom?"

"Finish your homework!"

3

Daddy's Little Girl

"Girls like to be played with, and rumpled a little too, sometimes."

—Oliver Goldsmith

I haven't reached that point in fathering yet when I'll wake up in a cold sweat worried there are boys out there thinking things about my sweet little girl like I thought about other people's sweet little girls.

If anything, when that time and day arrive, I hope to strike living terror in any teenager who darkens my doorstep—just like my father-in-law did to me.

I told my wife this once and she seemed shocked.

"What do you mean?!" my wife demanded.

I repeated myself: "I was afraid of your dad."

The man was, and still is, huge. He was the proverbial father teenagers would look at and say, "I'M GOING TO DIE!"

"But you were brave, for me," my wife said sweetly. "What did you do when you knocked on my door the first time? Did my dad answer?"

"All dads answer the door on first dates," I replied. "If I remember it right, my tongue swelled up in fear and I almost suffocated to death."

"Did my dad say anything to you?"

"No, he just stood there staring at me. I think he thought I was raising money door-to-door for the mute."

"Why do you think that?"

"He gave me a dollar."

"Well, apparently, you were okay—he let us go out, didn't he?"

"True," I replied. "But, before we left, he looked at me, then he looked at you, then he looked at my car."

"Why?"

"It was like he was telling me a little story through telepathy."

"What was the story about?"

"A horny high school student who now walks with a limp."

Her eyes flashed with a sudden realization. "Is that why you never held my hand in front of my dad?"

I nodded. "I was afraid he was going to say something."

"Like what?"

"Like, 'Hey, Romeo, freeze or I'll blow your head off!'"

Of course, our first date was nothing like a week later, when I went over to my future wife's house. It was the day before I was set to leave for spring vacation with my family. Her parents were gone, so, like high school kids do, we necked on the sofa.

Next thing I know, her parents are rolling into the driveway an hour earlier than planned. With my hair tousled, I start going nuts, shouting "Our Father, who art in Heaven," while she was spitting into her hand and smoothing down my cowlick.

As I was positioning myself on the couch to look as if I had been reading an interesting *National Geographic* article on apple maggots, her dad walks in the house and proceeds straight to the living room like a bounty hunter.

"Hi," I said, greeting him like a hoarse soprano. I would have also waved, but I got a paper cut from clutching the magazine like a life preserver, and I was trying to stop the bleeding with a linen doily.

Finally, as beads of sweat were rolling down my neck, the giant spoke in his deep, dark voice: "So, when are you leaving, Ken?"

"Right now," I answered, jumping up to go.

He looked at me for a moment and then started laughing. "I meant . . . on vacation."

"My dad still loves to talk about that," my wife remarked.

I can only hope to be half as scary when my daughter starts dating.

For now, however, my daughter is still flat chested and "definitely" not interested in boys—thank God! This doesn't mean, however, that my life is easy.

When my wife and I returned home from a night out recently, I heard a voice coming from the shadows at the top of the stairs: "Well, it's about time you got home! I thought you said you'd be back at 11:30—do you have any idea what time it is?!"

"Mom?" I shouted. "Is that you?" Peering into the dark, I exclaimed, "What are you doing in a Winnie the Pooh nightgown?"

"Very funny, Daddy," my daughter announced, as she bounded down the stairs and into my arms.

I braced myself for the third degree.

"What did you do tonight?" she asked.

"We went out to dinner with friends," I answered.

"Where?"

"A seafood restaurant."

"Why not Chuck E. Cheese? We always go to Chuck E. Cheese."

"I know, but your mom doesn't like to jump in the plastic balls wearing a skirt. She's very selfish."

My daughter sniffed my face. "You smell like smoke. Were you smoking?"

"No. But, other people were. Did you want to smell my breath, too?"

"Eeew. My teacher says secondhand smoke can kill you dead. It hurts."

"I know. Shouldn't you be in bed?"

"What did you have for dinner?" she continued, ignoring me.

"Oysters."

"Eeew! Do you like oysters?"

"No, but I like eating foods that trigger my gag reflex. Can't we . . ."

"What did Mom eat?"

I smiled. "That's a good question. I don't remember. Why don't you go find her and ask?"

"What did you have to drink?"

"Coffee. Is that okay with your teacher?"

"Do you like coffee?"

"No," I answered, "but it kills the taste of the oysters." I looked at my watch. "Aren't you supposed to be in bed? I didn't have to answer this many questions in high school when I came home late."

"Wait," she demanded. "I have one more question. What did you do after dinner?"

"We went to a movie," I said. "I had popcorn, your mom said she didn't want any, then ate half of mine. When the movie was over, we left. I'm wearing blue socks. It was an eighteen-mile round trip. Our friend's names are Bill and Sandi. And the movie was rated R—but we are all over the age of seventeen—I swear. Oh, and I had a breath mint before dinner. Anything else?"

"Were there any bad words in the movie?"

"Goodnight, sweetheart."

As I said this, my son wandered groggily into the room. "Did you have questions, too?"

"About what?" he asked.

"About when Mommy and I were gone."

"You were gone?"

"Forget it," I said, walking away.

I'm not sure which conversation was more disturbing.

As you can see, I have a talker in the family. This is especially distressing when driving in the car. If I hear "why" one more time, I'm searching out a military academy for my daughter and let the nation reap the benefits of a new weapon system far more powerful than an atom bomb. Let the next evil empire suffer the wrath of my little girl's questions. We can parachute her behind enemy lines and have her masquerade as the despotic ruler's daughter.

"Why are your uniforms gray? Why do you have a scar above your eye? Why do you want to invade Algeria?"

I would have to demand compensation from Uncle Sam because my daughter's training has been at the expense of my nerves:

Daughter: Where are we going?

Father: To see your aunt Ingrid.

Daughter: Why?

Father: She's sick.

Daughter: Why?

Father: She doesn't feel well.

Daughter: Why?

Father: *(Frustrated)* She has the clap.

Mother: Ken!

Father: She doesn't know what that means.

Daughter: Who clapped her?

Father: I'm kidding. She has pneumonia, sweetheart.

Daughter: What's pamonia?

Father: She got it from asking too many questions.

Daughter: No she didn't. Did she, Mom?

Mother: Honey, I'm driving.

Daughter: Why isn't Daddy driving?

Mother: Ken, you started this. Answer her.

Father: Claire, your mom is driving because Dad has a headache, which he's had for five years because he didn't ask his doctor enough questions.

Daughter: Does Uncle Dave have bamonia, or did he get clapped?

Mother: If she says that tonight at dinner with my mother there, you're in big trouble, Ken!

Father: Claire, just sit back and stop asking so many questions.

Daughter: Why is Daddy going to be in trouble?

Father: Claire!

Mother: Let's all play the quiet game.

Son: Yeah!

Daughter: How do you play it?

Mother: The first person to talk loses.

Daughter: Then do we play it again? When are we going to be there?

Father: *(Stern)* When we get there!

Daughter: Will I get polmovia or clapped?

Father: I WAS KIDDING!

Daughter: Aunt Ingrid isn't sick?

Father: Aunt Ingrid has pamonia . . . I mean pneumonia. She contracted it while working too many hours at the tire factory where she and Uncle Dave work. She expects to be better in two weeks and in the meantime is home in bed wearing a lavender nightgown and furry raccoon slippers. We will arrive at her house at approximately 5 P.M., upon which we will knock on the fake pine door and enter the house with the flowers we bought for $6.79. I am wearing blue socks, and your mother does not have any gum in her purse. You will fall asleep on the way home, and I will carry you up to your room and kiss you goodnight. The sun will rise at 6:30 A.M. and set around 6 P.M. That should answer all your questions.

Daughter: What color are the flowers?

Father: AAAggghhh!!

Son: Mom, when is my school play?

Father: Now don't you start with the questions, too!

Mother: Tomorrow night.

Daughter: He has a play?

Mother: Yes. Why?

Father: Why! Did you say why?!

Daughter: But what happens if we like the play?

Father: WHAT?!

Daughter: *(Crying)* If I clap, I'll get pamonia!

Besides these issues, I also have to wrestle with the fact that when my wife is away my daughter thinks she's my mother. Take, for example, the time my wife went to visit her sister for a week. My daughter asked if she and her brother could buy lunch all week.

I was offended. Was she saying I couldn't handle something as simple as making a school lunch?

I told my daughter, "Don't be ridiculous. I'd love to make your lunches." After all, how hard could it be? Every morning, I'd make them the same lunch I felt like eating that day, too. She looked skeptical when I told her this, but she always looks that way just before her mom leaves me in sole charge of her and her brother.

In this case, her concerns were justified. While I envisioned family unison around the breadboard, my daughter turned the chore into arbitration that would make a veteran labor mediator shudder.

On the first day, I woke up and decided I wanted a salami sandwich.

Claire, who had nervously lingered near the kitchen to watch me, argued that Mom would never make her eat lunch meat on a hot day.

"Duh." My son sighed.

After a 10-minute go-around, she settled for bagels and cream cheese. We next debated lettuce or sprouts until both kids missed their busses.

Despite this early setback, I was determined to persevere.

The next morning, I suggested bologna to my little girl and she said ham. I told her there wasn't ham in the house, but how about meat loaf? She asked for turkey.

The next two days were even worse.

By Thursday evening, I was all set to write a large enough check to the lunchroom lady to cover the kids until they left for college when, out of the blue, a little voice in my head inspired me to take one last stab at making lunches.

At 7 A.M. on the day my wife was set to return, I stood in the kitchen smiling from cheek to cheek at my daughter.

"So," I said buoyantly. "What would you like for lunch, sweetheart?"

She stared mistrustingly at me. "What do we have?"

"How about peanut butter and jelly?" I asked.

"I'd rather eat throw up."

The words *Let me stick my finger down my throat—you hold the bread* hung momentarily on my lips. "Tuna?"

"Tuna grosses me out."

"But a vomit sandwich doesn't? How about egg salad?"

She rolled her eyes: "The last time I ate THAT my friends wouldn't talk to me until I brushed my teeth . . . TWICE!"

I ordered her and her brother into the car. What happened next is still a blur. I made two maraschino cherry and melba toast sandwiches and threw them into the kids' lunchboxes.

As I walked into the house that evening, my wife stood holding the note my daughter brought home from school.

Dear Mr. Swarner,
Claire had an incident today during lunch. Apparently,
someone put a maraschino cherry and melba toast sandwich
in her lunchbox. It made her cry. She claimed you did this,
but I said it was probably your son playing a practical joke.
Not a nice trick to play on a thumb-sucker. I thought you'd
like to know. Yours truly, Ms. Goodesteem

My wife looked at me perplexed.

I debated whether to tell her that our daughter was trying to make me look stupid, but I figured she'd say I didn't need any help.

One of the fun parts of being a dad, however, is the hero worship you receive from your kids—heavy emphasis on the "you" receive. I, on the other hand, do not. And, quite frankly, it's been bothering me that my kids have never said they want to grow up to be a journalist like me.

It's not that they planned to be independently wealthy, living on some tropical island. My daughter stated she wants to be a teacher, and so does my son . . . just like their mother.

When I mentioned this to my wife, she said it's because the kids spend all day with teachers, and at their age, there is also an attraction to things maternal.

"I'm their father," I countered. "What's more attractive than that?"

"You're a dad."

"So?"

"So, I don't wake up the kids at 11 P.M. to show them the skyrocketing electricity bill."

"But my job is exciting," I argued. "Why don't they want to grow up and be like me?"

"You're a writer. What's so thrilling?"

"I left a preposition dangling the other day," I answered ominously. "Someone could have got hurt."

"Well, why don't you sign up for Take Your Daughter to Work Day?" she suggested. "Maybe if one of the kids saw what you did, you might gain more notoriety around here."

Now that was a great idea.

When the big day rolled around, I prepped my daughter as she ate her cereal.

"Now, honey," I said. "I want you to be prepared for anything today."

"Why?"

"Well, I have a demanding job," I said. "Things could get hairy."

"I thought you sat at your computer all day typing stories?"

"He does," my wife interrupted. "But he has a very uncomfortable chair."

I blanched. "Alright, let's go," I said moving toward the garage.

For the first hour of the morning, my daughter sat mesmerized at the edge of my desk, staring at me as I transcribed notes.

"Wow, you are really paying attention," I finally said. "Are you amazed at what I do here at work?"

"No," she stated. "I was just wondering if I'll have that much nose hair when I grow up."

During the second hour, she made pinwheels out of Post-its and paperclips.

Then, I took her to the cafeteria for lunch, and she sighed 17 times while my co-workers discussed football and television shows.

Finally, around 1 p.m., I received my big break. Firefighter Bob stopped by for an interview about National Stop, Drop, and Roll Day, and he gave my daughter a sticker and let her wear his badge.

My little girl's eyes were all lit up as she watched me interview him.

When we arrived home, my wife asked how things went.

"Great!" she exclaimed. "Dad interviewed a real live firefighter!"

As she ran upstairs to tell her brother, I turned to my wife. "On our way home, she said she wants to be a writer when she grows up."

"You must be very proud."

"Don't take it so hard," I chided her. "Your son still wants to be a teacher."

The next day at dinner, still feeling elated, I asked my daughter if she told the kids at school about her day yesterday.

"All of us who went to our parent's work had to give a report," she said.

"And?"

"Jason Roblee's dad works at the sewer department. He gets to trap rats and say the word *poop* whenever he wants," she said excitedly. "That's what I want to be when I grow up."

My wife smirked at me.

I shook my head. "How can I compete with that?!"

4

Go Ask Your Mother

One sunny day last summer, my kids walked into my den and asked, "Dad, can we play with the hose in the backyard?"

"I don't care," I said, thinking, *Since when do they ask?*

"Thanks," they chimed and ran outside.

A few minutes later, I caught a glimpse of my wife frantically running down the hall past my den. I can't confirm what happened when she reached the backyard, but according to my kids, she yelled, "Hit the dirt!" and dove on top of the sprinkler as if it were a hand grenade set to explode.

The kids were scrambling back into the house by the time I reached the back door.

"What are you doing?" I asked, as my wife was turning off the water spigot.

"Are you crazy letting them play with the water?!" she exclaimed, panting and out of breath.

"What's wrong?" I asked, removing the flecks of grass clippings that dotted her face.

She looked incredulously at me. "One drop of spray hits the power lines and your kids can forget about having normal offspring of their own!"

Every few weeks, it seems like I'm having a safety conversation with my wife, better known as Allison the Angst. Talk about paranoid: In the spring, she wanted all of us to wear matching solid red T-shirts at the county fair so no one would get lost.

"That's a great idea," I said. "Think how much that will ease our minds—until they announce over the loudspeaker: 'Would Tweedledee and Tweedledork please pick up your kids at Lost and Found.'"

I'm not sure why she is always worried that some disastrous accident will befall her family. I thought maybe something bad happened in her childhood. I've asked her if she was ever abandoned as a child.

"No," she answered.

"Run over?"

"No."

"Fallen from a hotel balcony? Slipped on some ice? Thrown from an elephant?"

"I'm not afraid of elephants," she argued.

"You cried on the Dumbo ride at Disneyland," I explained.

"You were flying it too high. Our son could have fallen out."

"How? You had him in a full nelson."

My wife frowned. "Someone has to be safety-conscious in this family."

"Sure, but does someone have to Heimlich her kids when they choke on water?"

"It's obvious you don't understand a mother's instinct," she huffed and walked out of the room.

That's true, I thought, *but it's really not worth arguing with her.* In fact, I told my son that when he asked if he could join the hockey team.

"What did your mother say?" I asked him.

"One slap-shot to the head and I'll be on life support until I'm eighty. Can't you give me permission to play?"

"If I do that, and you get hurt, I'll never hear the end of it. But look on the bright side," I told him. "Your mom says you can get out of your car seat when you're eleven."

"I'll believe it when I see it," he said, stomping off.

He's probably right.

It's not only my kids who suffer under my wife's "safety-conscious" regime—it also places a burden on our ability to get away. Until recently, she and I hadn't been alone for more than two days since the birth of our first child ten years ago. When an ad appeared in the Sunday travel section promoting a once-in-the-lifetime deal to cruise for seven days in Mexico, I couldn't resist. I booked the cruise, bought a sailor's hat, and surprised my wife.

At first she was excited, dancing around the room like a giddy schoolgirl on the last day of class before summer vacation. Then, like a gray cloud snuffing out the sun, her face dropped as she realized she'd be separated from our children for more than forty-eight hours.

After a lot of coaxing—and even some pleading—she eventually consented to the trip, and before I knew it, we were standing on the gangplank waving good-bye to our kids—who, quite honestly, were more than happy to be spoiled by Grandma and Grandpa for a week.

Needless to say, my wife worried constantly about the children. Every time our feet stepped on dry land during the cruise, she wanted to call them—sometimes twice in the same day.

So it seemed rather routine near the end of the vacation as we both squeezed into a phone booth on the dock in Cabo.

I dialed the phone, and when my mom answered, I gave another hearty hello from Mexico, and she responded with those dreaded words, "I don't want to ruin your vacation, but . . ."

I chose to keep my smile plastered on my face so not to alarm my wife, but I was dying inside.

"Really," I said with as much enthusiasm as I could muster. "What's up?"

My mom explained that my son fell down on his face while playing tag around the playground equipment.

"And?" I continued.

"And there is no reason to worry," she answered. "He's perfectly fine—the CAT scan didn't turn anything up."

I wanted to say, "Did you say CAT scan?" But exactly how do you say CAT scan without it sounding like you're saying, "WILL HE LIVE?"

Suddenly, all the begging and pleading I did to go on this trip were boiling in my stomach. I felt like I kidnapped my wife, fully knowing my son would bite it on the Big Toy. It's not like I could continue standing there smiling, either. There's nothing worse than smiling—unless, of course, if your wife sees you smiling—as you say, "Did he have a concussion?"

Before I could say or do anything though, my wife's sixth sense for horrible things befalling her family kicked in and she asked, "Is everything alright?"

I nodded an unconvincing "yes" while on the other end of the phone my mom was explaining the scrapes and contusions around my son's right eye.

That's when I completely lost it. "So, good news?" I blurted out. "He didn't need stitches?"

"STITCHES?!" my wife shouted.

In retrospect, I think I could have handled that better. Maybe I should have eased into the whole thing more gently. For example, I could have said to my mom, "So he's having a good time, minus the bleeding?" Or, "So you guys ran some errands, visited the emergency room, and then stopped for soft-serve?"

The moment I said "stitches," however, the phone was yanked from my hands and I was pushed aside.

Of course, everything worked out, my son was fine, and a few days later we were all reunited. My wife even said she and I are going to go on another vacation—just the two of us— probably after the kids have graduated from college—grand-kids that is.

I have to admit, though, it's not easy being a mom. I know— my wife tells me that every day. She tells me that moms shoulder a great burden to make sure their kids have clean underwear, say polite things, make friends, and represent the family's "good" name.

With my wife, though, you have to add on top of that at least three layers of antiseptic.

Take my son's first day of kindergarten. I walked down the stairs to find him lined up at the front door as his mom ran over last-minute details.

"What's the most important thing about nap time?" she asked him.

"That we have our own mat for the entire year," my son answered.

"Why?"

"Bed wetters."

"Right." She smiled. "Do you sit on the toilet seats?"

"Not unless I have a death wish."

"Good. How about gifts from friends?"

He thought for a moment. "Oh, yeah—no accepting gum that's already been in someone's mouth?"

"And?"

"Avoid the kids who eat their boogers."

She looked proudly at me. "I think he's ready."

"For what?" I asked. "The next bubonic plague outbreak?"

My wife gave me that "if it weren't for moms, dads would accidentally kill their kids" look. She reached into her purse and handed my son a piece of paper.

"Here you go, Alasdair. Here are the numbers to Daddy's office, cell phone, pager, voice mail, e-mail, and the pay phone at Mr. Wong's Take-Out." She pinned the list to his sweater.

"Why are you giving him all of that?" I asked her.

"In case he can't reach me."

"Why would he call?"

"He might have a question or a problem."

"What does that mean?" I exclaimed. "I'll be getting calls at work from a child whose pant's zipper is stuck?"

"I'm trying to cover all the bases."

"Then why don't you just sit in class with him for the first few days?" I asked.

"Do you think they'd let me?"

"Sure, as long as you agree to raise your hand and nap quietly with the other children."

Ignoring me, my wife finished packing our son's backpack. Unfortunately, the backpack was so full of stuff, when he slung it on his back, he toppled right over.

I stood there looking at my son flailing his legs in the air like an upside-down turtle.

"I put two of everything in there, just in case he loses the first," my wife said matter-of-factly.

I kept my mouth shut as we walked out the door.

At the school, my wife hovered over our son as we stepped up to the classroom door. She ran over all the last-minute details with him: manners, hygiene, things stuck to the bottom of his shoes. Then, as we introduced ourselves to the kindergarten teacher, Ms. Goodesteem, a strange look came over the teacher's face.

"Wow, that's quite a big backpack you have, Alasdair," Ms. Goodesteem said to my son.

I smiled at the teacher. "He's climbing Everest after lunch."

The teacher looked curiously at me for a moment, then bent down to greet another child.

"Alright, Alasdair, it's time you go into class," I said.

"Mphrph."

"Excuse me?"

He gulped. "I said, I can't breathe."

I loosened my wife's grip around his body. "Okay, dear, you're choking our son."

She finally let go, and our kindergartner bounded excitedly into his classroom.

After a couple minutes, I said, "Honey, we should go."

"Just one more minute," she pleaded, refusing to budge from the classroom window.

"Okay," I replied, "but stop smashing your face against the window—it's scaring the thumb-suckers."

She looked over at me with tears in her eyes. "He's growing up."

"Yep," I answered. "Kindergarten is a big step to take."

"I know," she replied. "I hope he's going to be alright."

I laughed. "I meant for you."

I just wish I could be so understanding with my wife when it comes to household chores.

Every Saturday morning it's the same routine: Reveille at 7 A.M. followed by a quick breakfast, then formation and the doling out of assigned duties. The kids and I stand there with our chests puffed out and our knees locked wondering where we could hide.

"Okay, listen up!" my wife shouts. "Ken, you have the kitchen this morning. I want the floors waxed, the oven cleaned, and don't brush those bread crumbs into the Tupperware drawer again!"

"Yes, dear."

"Alasdair, I'm on to you, son. I know you're hiding your dirty socks somewhere. And, Claire, I have only two words for you: sticky walls. So, here are your tool belts, your time cards, and your pagers—let's get going—and no loafing!"

Ten hours later we were done.

Last weekend, our routine took a definite turn for the worse. My wife started the morning by banging pots and pans with a wooden spoon yelling, "Get up and smell the Soft Scrub!"

"Don't we ever get a week off?" I moaned, rubbing the sleep out of my eyes.

"You did last year," she answered.

"You mean after my vasectomy?"

"Yeah."

"You still made me polish the silverware," I stammered.

"So?"

"So, I was in a fetal position."

She chuckled. "You got off easy."

"I cried."

"Okay, enough chitchat!" she yelled. "Half the day's over."

"This is ridiculous. It's five in the morning!"

"Cleanliness is next to Godliness," she said.

"Oh yeah, so tell me, Saint Spit and Polish, who are we trying to impress?"

"A new family moved into the neighborhood yesterday," she answered.

"They're having their housewarming party here?"

"No, but what if they drop by unexpectedly?"

"You always worry about that, but no one ever does," I declared. "Just their kids do."

"And what will they say when their parents quiz them about our place?"

"That you made them wear surgical booties over their shoes?"

"No, that we have a nice, clean home."

"And children notice that?" I asked.

"Our kids do."

"Our kids are hiding in the attic."

"So that's where they are! (*Yelling*) Alright you slackers, you've got extra sweeping duty for this!"

Aren't there labor laws against this sort of thing?

Of course, the only thing worse than cleaning is the prelude to October 31. It started this year on the 4th of July—even though my wife promised me things would be different this time.

I should have expected it. At 7 P.M., as the red smoke bomb blew white vapor over the fence and set off the neighbor's fire alarm, I saw my wife's vacant lawn chair with a plate of uneaten potato salad perched on the armrest and I felt an all-too-familiar uneasiness.

"Where's your mom?" I asked the children. "She's going to miss the Smoking Joe's Cabin."

"She yelled something about 119 days and ran into the house," my son reported.

The match I was holding burned down to my thumb. "Oh, no!"

As the smoking cabin burst into a three-alarm blaze, I stormed into my wife's sewing room and found her rummaging in a box of yarn. "You're kidding yourself, you know," I said. "Now come out and enjoy the fireworks."

"I can't," she cried. "Halloween is less than four months away. I have to start making the kids' costumes."

I pulled her out of the closet.

"I'm not leaving them to the last minute," she said loosening herself from my grip.

I laughed portentously. "You say that every year, and every year you finish them at 6 P.M., October 31st. Now c'mon."

She grabbed her shearing scissors and backed against the wall.

"Honey," I said soothingly. "Put down the scissors or I'll call S.W.A.T."

She threw them to the left, and as I bent down to get them, she did an end run, grabbed her sewing kit, and took off toward the backyard.

By the time I was back outdoors, she had the porch light trained on my son's small face and was grilling him in her best Joe Friday voice: "And what do you want to be for Halloween?"

He shrugged.

She told him to think "long and hard about his future" and then she tied my daughter to her lawn chair. "What do you want to be, sweetie?"

I hurried over and lit the Flaming Pinwheel I had nailed to

the elm tree. As it ignited the bark, I yelled: "Look everyone, the fireworks are over here!"

Have you ever tried to draw attention away from a grown woman browbeating children with bunny ears, fake vampire blood, and a trunkload of sewing patterns?

"Maybe they should go as tortured political prisoners," I suggested.

"Don't listen to your father," my wife told the kids. "Grandma made his Halloween costume with a blanket."

I put a sparkler in each of my kids' trembling hands. "Honey, it's too much pressure."

"No! They must decide what they want to be right now. I have to get started!"

Finally, I lost it. "Why don't you just buy their costumes?!" The words seemed to echo against the black sky.

My wife did a double take and spit fire. "My mother never just BOUGHT a costume!"

"Is that why we don't go over to her house for the 4th of July?"

Ignoring me, she grabbed up the kids and carried them into the house to measure their inseams.

I extinguished the tree, boxed up the remaining fireworks, and put them in the garage next to the leftovers from the last 4th.

I think I'll have next year's promise notarized.

Of course, what's more amazing was my son's actions last Halloween even though he knows his mother as well as anyone. I knew there'd be trouble the moment he opened his mouth when she asked him what he wanted to be for Halloween.

"Jason," he answered.

"Jason, who?" she asked.

"The guy who cuts up people with a chain saw."

I stepped in immediately. "How about we all sit down and discuss this?"

My wife looked shocked. "Last year he wanted to be a dog," she mumbled as I led her to the couch. "With cute little spots and a gabardine collar."

I held her for a moment. "Honey," I said. "Alasdair is growing up."

She looked at our son. "Don't you want to be a dog again?" she asked.

"Dalmatians aren't cool, Mom," he answered.

"How about a Great Dane?" she retorted. "With a spike collar?"

He shook his head. "I want to be a real person this year, not an animal."

"That sounds reasonable," I interjected.

My wife's face brightened. "That's fine. You could go as a pilgrim."

"What?!" my son shrieked. "Mom, I could get beat up for doing that."

She looked shocked. "You could?"

I nodded. "Yeah, smocks aren't cool in the fourth grade."

"Why can't I be Jason, or a monster, or something?" he asked.

"It's just that I don't like the violence these costumes represent," she explained. "They are so dark and morbid."

My son's shoulders sank. We sat in silence for a few moments.

"You know," I said, "we could put a different spin on things."

"How do we do that?" she asked.

"Easy," I answered. "He could dress up as a happy mutant. His face could be melting off, but he's okay with it."

"Ken!"

"No really. We could add blush to his sagging face and have him sing a couple show tunes."

"I don't want to sing any show tunes," my son replied.

"Do you want the scar stuff and tube of fake blood?" I asked.

"Yeah."

"Then you'll run around with your chain saw singing 'The Sun'll Come Out Tomorrow.'"

My wife shook her head. "I'm not comfortable with this."

"Would you prefer something from *Cats*?"

My wife stood up and exclaimed, "Am I the only one in this room who thinks there is enough violence in the world already? Do we really need to dress up our babies as serial killers so they can perpetuate the violent, socially demented, and awful acts of dehumanization that exist on this earth?"

"No," I replied. "I'm pretty much against that stuff, too. How about he goes as Frankenstein's Monster, who feels so blessed to be alive again that he joins the clergy? We could tape a priest collar around the bolts in his neck."

"Cool!" my son exclaimed.

My wife walked out of the room without a word.

Later, my son told me that he agreed to be a pilgrim. "Mom said I can carry a gun."

"A musket," she said. "Pilgrims shot small game, you know."

After my son left the room, I looked at her. "Very slick. What are you going to do next year?"

She frowned. "Think I can convince him to be a postman if I let him have a letter opener?"

I just nodded.

———————

I noticed the warning signs immediately. My wife, hunched over the counter with a frantic look in her eyes, a stack of photos, and tacky glue.

She was obsessing again.

This time her all-engrossing project has been completing the children's Memory Books—you know, those scrapbooks with the categories you're supposed to fill in for each year of their lives. The ones where you write their height and weight, who their friends were, where they went on vacation, and what their favorite color was. It's a classic baby shower gift.

For the past ten years, our son's and daughter's Memory Books have occupied shelf space next to the photo albums. Reading my son's book, I can tell you everything about him . . . until he was two. He liked patty cake, his first birthday cake was Dalmatians, and he cried during his first haircut.

Glancing through my daughter's book, ALL I can tell you is that whoever bought us the book left the receipt in it.

I should have known this wouldn't last. Eventually my wife was bound to snap and finish the books—hunker down with vats of coffee—clear her calendar for a couple weeks—tell her family "it's now or never." It's just like last year when she decided to update ten years of photo albums in one month. She lost eleven pounds, and the kids and I moved into a hotel.

When I walked into the kitchen and saw the Memory Books taken down from the shelf, I didn't hesitate—I made backup reservations at the Hilton. The kids wept.

"Is Mommy going to start mumbling to herself again?" my daughter asked.

"I don't know," I replied. "Let's hold hands and pray."

Just as I expected, so much time has passed since the kids

were born that many of the memories for the Memory Books are blurred. This, however, has not deterred my wife. Throughout the day, when you least expect it, she attacks.

"Ken, what was your son's favorite song in the first grade?"

"I'M IN THE SHOWER!" I shouted.

"Ken, when did our daughter stop sucking her thumb?"

"Honey, it's 3 A.M."

"Ken, what were our son's first words?"

"I'll tell you when I free my finger from this bike chain!"

Yesterday, I couldn't take it any longer. "Why don't you ask your kids?" I exclaimed.

"I have," she replied. "But they're so tired of my questions—I think they're making things up so I'll leave them alone. Your son says he started shaving when he was five—that can't be right, can it?"

I was about to suggest counseling when her face perked up. "Guess what I just remembered? I bet the pediatrician has the kids' weights and heights since they were toddlers. I think I'll go call him."

I blanched. "Oh, honey, don't call the dentist . . . he's in my Rotary Club. Let's keep this our little secret."

About this time my son walked into the room.

"I know something you could write in my book," he announced.

My wife's eyes glistened. "Oh good, I knew you'd come around."

He cleared his throat. "Write this under most embarrassing memory in 2001: 'The time my mom called my old day care to ask when I stopped walking around with my hand down my pants.'"

My wife frowned. "They couldn't remember."

I gave my wife a hug and told her that if the kids and I remember anything else for the Memory Books, we'd send a postcard from the Hilton.

With that said, the Martha Stewart I live with still has her share of blue days . . . from the middle of June until school starts again.

Something unusual happens to my wife in the summer. A person who is an active and busy parent throughout the school year, who is self-assured and occupied, suddenly turns to Jell-O when she and her children are home to roost 24 hours a day.

To cope, she calls me.

"Ken," she said recently, "if you really loved me, you'd come home right now and take the children for a very long drive."

"Allison, it's 10 in the morning."

"I know, but they made a hammock with our shower curtain."

The fact that I have a job and boss are often lost on her.

"Sweetheart, what am I supposed to say to the boss: 'I've got to go, my wife is under attack from the Lollipop Gang—if I'm not back in three hours, send reinforcements'?"

Unfortunately, this seems perfectly reasonable to her. And considering that I am sequestered away at a quiet office with other adults all summer long, it's difficult to portray these phone calls as major problems, especially when my wife calls to say one of our children dumped bumblebees into the mailbox and they stung the postman.

Luckily for me, there are other dads at work who have the same dilemma, so we started an ad hoc support group. It's nothing formal, we just keep an eye out for each other when the phone rings so no one is trapped listening to forty-five minutes of: "Do you know what YOUR children are doing right now?!"

Club members do the following . . .

Screen phone calls.

Jim: "Hi, Allison. No this is Jim. Ken can't come to the phone right now—I think he's in the bathroom. He had fried food again—I told him not to . . . Yep, I don't expect him out until 5. Okay, bye-bye."

Provide humanitarian assistance.

Joe: "Hurry, someone smash my hands in this file cabinet so I can't pick up the phone anymore!"

Jim: "Sure, as long as you punch me really hard in the stomach so I can't talk."

Cover each other when the boss is suspicious.

Boss: "Who is Ken talking to?"

Jim: "A client."

Boss: "Then why is he telling the client to send the kids to their rooms?"

Jim: "Uh, it's our new customer service program?"

Boss: "Our new policy is to discipline other people's children?"

Jim: "Yes, but don't worry, we charge extra for spankings."

Counsel each other.

Ken: "Okay Jim, repeat after me: 'The phone is not my enemy. I am not afraid of the phone.'"

We even have secret hand signs when on the phone.

One finger means "I'm fine, I can handle this."

Two fingers mean "Create a diversion in five minutes."

Three fingers mean "Hurry, grab my phone and yank it from the wall!"

Of course, when no one is around, we have to rely on our

own wits—like the time I told my wife: "Honey, I've got to go, Joe just told me that Frank in Marketing is on fire."

I wonder if my boss would consider an unlisted number here at work?

For Mother's Day, my daughter's class had to compile reasons why their moms should be president of the United States. Of course, they did this by drawing pictures with crayons.

I got to thinking how Claire might write an essay about her mom as the commander-in-chief. Here's what she probably would say:

> My name is Claire, I'm eight, and I'd like you to elect my mom president of the United States. It would be a nice Mother's Day gift because my dad said she'd get a raise, and she deserves one after taking care of a house, kids, and phone solicitors from vinyl siding companies.
>
> Why should you vote for my mom? She's really smart. She's had the same job for twelve years. She can do lots of things at the same time like cook dinner, organize my Girl Scout hike, and ask my brother if he's going to take out the garbage before it "finally" spills over and kills someone. If she was president, she'd probably put her hands on her hips a lot, too, and ask: "Am I the only government employee who picks up her things instead of leaving them around the White House? Do I have to be president *and* your maid?!"
>
> I've heard some presidents and their families have done bad things and embarrassed the American people. Don't worry about my family. My mom makes us go to church every Sunday, send thank-you cards after birthdays, and brush our teeth before bed. She even tells my dad not to

swear if my brother and I accidentally ride our bikes over the sprinkler heads.

Oh, and for really big, fancy parties at the White House, my mom will make sure her family is dressed nicely; even my dad, who my mom says has a hard time wearing things that match.

There will be some drawbacks when she is elected. If *Air Force One* isn't working, it will take her a while to get across the country in her little blue Hyundai. And if she has to choose between attending my school play or defending our Southern border—good-bye Texas.

My dad says presidents need to campaign on the issues. They need to stand for something. I suppose my mom is for the following:

Clean environment—I'm not allowed to feed squirrels gum.

Healthy foods—She says eating chocolate in the morning gives you worms.

Stern education—She has a sixth sense when I haven't done my homework.

Strong police—She's not afraid to bring in the big guns: my dad!

Safe living—I'll be in a car seat until I'm sixteen.

In addition, she's strict about bedtimes, running in the house, sunscreen, and she doesn't let my dad put his feet on the coffee table (my grandma says Martha Washington would turn in her grave if my dad lived in the White House—whatever that means).

Finally, my grandpa told me presidents make promises they don't keep. Not my mom. If she says she'll give you something to cry about, she's not kidding.

So please vote for my mom. My dad says the country could use a good mother.

5

Father Knows Least

"Becoming a father is easy enough,
But being one can be rough."

—Wilhelm Busch

Before my wife left town to visit her sister, she told me she didn't want to come home to a huge pile of laundry . . . again.

Having seen this expression on her face before, I played it safe and told her I would stay on top of it. *What's a little laundry?* I thought.

Unfortunately, the moment she left, the kids started changing their outfits three or four times a day . . . or so it seemed. I swear that every time I got the laundry caught up, thirty minutes later, the laundry room looked like a place to train mountain climbers. Once, a fast-moving avalanche of whites buried the cat and I had to get a snow shovel to save her.

I kept thinking how disappointed my wife would be to see the laundry out of control, so to compensate, I instituted new rules in the house.

"Until your mom returns," I told the kids, "you have to spot clean all minor stains rather than dump them in the laun-

dry room, and at the end of the day, unless your clothes are beyond hope, refold them and put them back in your dressers."

I even played recorded subliminal messages under their
beds at night: "If it smells clean, it probably is." "No one will
notice that stain." "If it doesn't have skid marks, give it another day!"

Of course, I have discovered that it's not easy for children to
monitor their clothing use. My daughter complained that she
was being unfairly forced to make tough decisions like how
much spaghetti sauce on a shirt warrants a washing.

"Is it a dab?" she asked. "A couple spots? An entire left
sleeve?!"

As their father, I'm doing my best to help them. For three
nights, the kids lined up in the hall as I walked down the line
examining their clothes. It worked pretty well—except the
time my son's socks made me vomit.

But don't get me wrong, the kids supported my efforts to
keep up on the laundry. It's just that their mom taught them to
always put their clothes in the hamper at the end of the day—
so they were understandably a little confused. They felt better
one morning, though, when I said their mom would be home
in a few days. That eased their minds . . . as I lined the children up at the front door and I sprayed down their clothes
with Lysol.

Unfortunately, my son forgot to cover his face during the
spray-down, and he went to school with bloodshot eyes. He
told me that by the look on his teacher's face, she thought he
had a drug problem.

"Just because your eyes were a little red?" I scoffed.

"That," he said, "and because I was wearing the same shirt
for a third straight day."

I told him that he made me proud.

I was a little concerned that the kids were going to crack under the pressure before their mom came home and start wearing green trash bags to save themselves the agony. How would I explain that to their school principal?

"Well, you see, Ms. Winterbottom, we're trying to reduce the amount of laundry at home so I don't end up in the nuthouse, mumbling the names of laundry detergents to my roommate."

It's probably best that my wife came home. On the last night she was gone, my son caught me examining his underwear with a magnifying glass.

Sleep, I have decided, is the most important activity in a dad's life. It outranks baseball, junk food, and a night out with the guys—in terms of helping one get through life, that is.

Fathers can't own this tool, however. In fact, I haven't had a good night's sleep since 1990.

It's really no wonder then that I am a zombie at work—floating along the workforce like kelp in the ocean.

It's not fair how the corporate world expects so much from the parents it employs. How can I be expected to compete in this age of maximum-productivity with the amount of sleep I get at home?

Childless employees and employers don't understand this, either. They look at me as if I was in control of my sleep patterns. A recent staff meeting at work exemplified this rift.

The meeting began shortly after 11 A.M., and it was pleasant enough in the beginning. We were huddled to discuss a big, important project that all the big-wigs upstairs had thrown at our department to complete. Apparently, the fact that I was in my chair didn't impress the others in the room.

"Ken, are you alright?" my boss asked.

"What? Yes, I was just thinking," I said, noticing all the eyes in the room were on me.

"With your head on the table and your eyes closed?"

"Ah, ah, well," I stammered, "I was concentrating . . . you know, nose to the grindstone kind of stuff."

"You were drooling," he said.

"I'm excited about this project—that's all!" I exclaimed pointing at the paper in front of me.

"That's a take-out menu from Wongs," he replied. "We were about to order lunch."

I looked in shock at the pompous faces around the table. The childless suits smirked at me as if I were a schoolboy caught daydreaming; everyone, that is, except for Sam from Accounting, a father of four who was holding a bottle of Wite-Out to his nose to stay awake.

"Am I . . . am I in the right room?" I asked, pretending I had amnesia.

It's amazing how sleep deprivation can alter your state of being. I used to be Johnny-on-the-spot at work—climbing the corporate ladder two rungs at a time. I was the first to arrive and the last to leave. I even worked in my dreams.

Then, I merged my life with a child, and now all I can do is . . . dream. It all started when the sleeping arrangement at home changed. You see, in the middle-of-the-night pecking order, I'm chomped.

Here's a typical night at my house:

10:30 P.M.: My wife and I—too exhausted to floss, occasionally penciling in a kiss but typically making only eye contact like two tortured lab animals—slump off to sleep, sometimes with the stove burner left on.

12:30 A.M.: My son trudges off to the bathroom, misses the toilet bowl I have strung with runway lights, pelts the cat in the eye, then knees my groin as he climbs onto my side of the bed.

1 A.M.: Trapped in the middle and asphyxiated from bad first-grader breath, I burrow under my wife and pop up at the edge of the bed barely alive. The rapid movement of fresh air, however, knocks me back to sleep.

1:45 A.M.: Dreaming of climbing to the top of an Ivy League football dog pile, I awake to discover my son trapped under my pillow . . . whimpering.

2:15 A.M.: My daughter, who I never heard come into my bed, yells as if possessed: "Daddy, get out. It's too crowded." I nudge my wife to move; she won't, so I leave.

2:25 A.M.: After removing seven layers of toys with a snow shovel, I climb under my daughter's Barbie comforter and, with my feet sticking out, fall back to sleep.

2:40 A.M.: I wake up with my daughter's bottom in my face. I push it away and she cries, "Daddy, stop it. I'm trying to sleep." I get out of her bed and limp to the kitchen to de-ice my toes over the stove burner.

2:55 A.M.: I slump off to my son's Ferrari bed and dive into three feet of water. I grab a leaking water pistol to stay afloat and hoist myself out.

2:57 A.M.: Drying off with a Tickle Me Elmo, I land on the lumpy living room couch, my head sloping a foot below my feet. As the blood rushes to my eyeballs, I start my mental to-do list. Number one: Make appointment with chiropractor.

3:30 A.M.: The phone rings. With my brain swimming in

blood, I reach for it and fall off the narrow couch and onto my daughter curled up on the floor. "Daddy! I'm trying to sleep!" The phone stops ringing before I can get to it.

3:34 A.M.: I slip under a pile of laundry on the family room couch and I'm lulled to sleep by chirping birds and automatic lawn sprinklers.

5 A.M.: Peeking through my son's Batman underwear, I watch as my children peel the clothes off the pile until they reach my exhausted body: "We're hungry. Make us breakfast!" they chime. Before I can answer, they begin to cry, which inspires all the dogs in the neighborhood to bark.

6 A.M.: The paperboy pelts my sleeping face with the morning edition, and I fall off the milk box.

You can see my weekdays are hopeless. But even the busiest, most sleep-deprived human beings should receive time on the weekends to rejuvenate, right? A little extra sleep on a Saturday morning would go a long way in regaining my stature.

I've explained this to my children.

"Kids, Daddy has worked hard all week long. In between important corporate meetings, I've run car pool, I retrieved your kite out of the tree with only a minor cut and sprained ankle, I've led Cub Scout sing-a-longs, and I've sold 20 candy bars for the soccer team. All I am asking now is to sleep to 9 A.M. tomorrow morning. Will you let me do this?"

They nod.

Next morning, 6 A.M., a child taps on my eyelids with a grapefruit spoon.

"Ugh!"

"Dad, did I wet my bed?" a tiny voice asks.

"What?"

"I mean, it's wet. Do you think I did?"

"How would I know?" I complain.

"Could you come and smell it?"

Am I really having this conversation? "You promised to let me sleep!" I whine. "Go away."

In a huff, the child retreats.

A few minutes later, a small, ice-cold hand reaches into my mouth, and a voice shouts, "WHAT DOES MY HAND TASTE LIKE?!"

There is something about a sleeping dad that kids can't tolerate. We are like a menace to their world. Maybe that's why some mornings, if I ignore their attempts to wake me, the children will change tactics and invade with tall ladders and a battering ram. One child sits on the catapult while the other cuts the cord, launching the first through the air and onto my groin.

"Are you awake?" my son asks.

"Do it again. Maybe he didn't feel it," my daughter chimes in.

"Why is he making that funny puffing noise?"

I lie motionless, the wind knocked out of me, hoping they'll give me up for dead. They don't. My only defense has been to push them on top of their mother (chivalry is dead before sunup). But that doesn't work—they just roll right off and run back around to jump on me again.

Finally, in order to maintain the pretense that I am in charge and that sleeping in is my right, the children are banished to their rooms for all eternity. On the surface this might sound good, but the children (who are taught this on the playground by big kids) fight back by opening their doors every five minutes to ask, "Can we come out now?"

You'd think I would be immune to all this by now, but, like a deadly virus, my children have learned to adapt to my world and increase in their intensity.

Like recently, for example. At 5:45 A.M., standing behind the moat I dug the previous evening, my kids whispered, "Psst, hey Dad, the invasion's called off. So can we go make ourselves breakfast?"

"Whatever," I moaned, barely conscious.

(A long pause). "Thanks." I heard them drop their swords and scurry off down the hall.

Suddenly, it was quiet for the first time in ten years. My dream came true. I scrunched back down under the covers, snuggling up to my wife. Moments later I was dreaming of places kids aren't allowed to go.

Then my eyes flipped open. It was too quiet.

I jumped over the moat and padded to the kitchen. I found them standing on two chairs stacked on top of each other, reaching for the glass cereal bowls.

"Hi, Dad," they shouted. "Since you're up, can you make us bacon?"

I wonder if there's something in workers' compensation that covers this?

I also wonder why I can't even get a break on Father's Day.

Two years ago, I was awoken by a loud crash downstairs.

"What was that?" I asked my wife.

"Either the dog just chased a large cat through the doggie door, or the kids are making you breakfast in bed for Father's Day."

A little while later, my two darling mop-headed children walked into the bedroom holding a large tray of food at a dangerous angle with an orange juice glass tipped over and leaking onto the floor . . . make that my bed . . . or rather, me.

"Breakfast is served!" my son announced with dramatic flair.

I stared at the tray.

"Go ahead, Daddy, eat up!" my daughter explained.

"Now?" I replied, staring at a lump of blackened toast. "It's really too pretty to eat—maybe I could shellac the whole thing and keep it on my desk next to the God's eye you made me last year."

"Nooooo," they chimed on key. "Eat it now."

I grabbed the spoon and paused. "Is that grapefruit juice on my cereal?"

"Yea," my son replied. "There wasn't enough milk for our breakfast and yours."

I dipped my spoon in, closed my eyes, and took a bite. "Mmm—cereal that makes your face pucker."

The kids beamed with pride.

"They should market this," I told my wife with a pained expression on my face. "It's for people who like it when their eyes water."

"I hope it's good," my son interjected. "I had a lot of trouble opening the plastic bag inside the cereal box, and it all exploded out of the box."

"All of it?" I asked. "So, what's this I'm eating?"

"The parts the dog couldn't get. We swept it into your bowl."

My daughter nodded enthusiastically.

I investigated my cereal. "Well, that certainly explains the bread clip, dog hair, and . . . what's this?"

My son examined my spoon. "A raisin—can you believe all of that was under the refrigerator?"

I sat frozen in shock.

"By the way, I lost a nickel under there last week," my son said. "I get it back if it's in there."

"I think I'm going to be sick," I said.

My wife glanced over the edge of the bed. "The dog doesn't look good, either."

Of course, this year, the same thing happened again—I was awoken to slamming cupboards and the smell of burnt toast.

I rolled over and looked at my wife. "Honey, I don't think I can stomach another bowl of whatever rolled under the fridge this year."

"You'll just have to be brave," she retorted. "You can't disappoint them."

"True, but if I eat a bug or something, won't it be more disappointing for them to watch Daddy lapse into a coma?"

"What do you suggest?" she asked.

"I could pretend that during the night my throat swelled up and I can't eat," I said. "As the kids round the corner, you could tell them that I was stung by a giant mosquito."

"They won't buy it."

"How about you rush downstairs and tell the kids *you'll* make breakfast?"

"And spoil their fun?" she asked shaking her head and leaving the room.

"Where are you going at a time like this?" I shouted after her. "Come back and help me eat the stray twisties and dust bunnies . . . Okay? . . . I'll pay you . . . hello?"

Next year, I'm sweeping under the fridge before it's too late.

Speaking of Father's Day, isn't it funny how soon your kids turn on you?

Last June, at the breakfast table, when I asked my son to pass the syrup, he said, "Why, because it's Father's Day?"

"No, because it's in your hand."

Passing it, he complained, "Gosh, when is Kid's Day?"

I did a double take. "When I was a kid and your grandma heard me say that, she'd yell: 'Every day is Kid's Day!'"

"Grandma can't hear," he argued.

"Before that."

"Well, it's not true," he continued. "You get to do whatever you want, whenever you want, and we don't."

"Yeah," my daughter chimed in.

"Then I'd like to sit on the porch and watch you guys mow the lawn."

"I can't reach the handle on the mower," my son said.

"Have I made my point?"

He frowned. "I suppose this means you get the last pancake, too?"

My kids are so focused on all the "have"s I have that they fail to recognize the stress and toil that come with it. They have no idea how tough it is to be a dad. That's why, I suppose, on Father's Day, they acted as if I didn't need the extra notoriety.

I wasn't surprised when my son walked into the garage later that day:

"Dad, what are you doing?"

"Banging my head on my steering wheel," I answered.

"You're so lucky you get to drive."

"I just backed over my wheelbarrow."

"You can fix it, Dad. You have all the really cool tools."

"You left it behind my car."

"I wish I had a car."

"It dented my bumper and popped my rear tire."

"I wish I could change a tire."

"My insurance company isn't going to be happy," I said.

"Yeah, but they'll do what you say." *(Rolling his eyes)* "Everyone does."

"Son, I'm going to go inside now and throw up."

"I wish I was allowed to use the downstairs bathroom."

"Or maybe I'll just lie down right here and cry."

"I wish I could relax."

I guess the whole human race depends on this have-and-have-not relationship. After all, if our kids really knew what we went through, would any of them sign up to be a dad?

A classic example of this is our nightly bedtime routine:

At 6:30 P.M.: with the dinner dishes cleared away, and the food under my son's chair licked up by the dog, I lay down the law, instructing the children to finish their homework, take their baths, read, and go to bed.

6:35 P.M.: I remind my son to stop jumping on the couch.

6:36 P.M.: I remind my son to stop jumping on the couch.

6:45 P.M.: My daughter cries because she doesn't understand her homework. Yet every time I explain how to do it, she's too busy singing, or sticking a pen in her ear, or falling off the back of her chair.

6:47 P.M.: I remind my son to stop jumping on the couch.

6:53 P.M.: While holding my daughter on her chair with my knee, I catch a glimpse of my wife silently moving down the hall as if making a break for it. I make a mental note: "Next time, escape first."

6:59 P.M.: My son executes a double gainer, rebounds off the couch cushion, and knocks the cat off the piano bench. "I'm doing my homework!" he exclaims as I round the corner.

7 P.M.: I pop a couple aspirin.

7:09 P.M.: I finally find my wife hiding in the linen closet—she refuses to come out until the children are asleep.

7:14 P.M.: In between coloring her toenails with a permanent marker and fighting with her brother, my daughter cries that she STILL doesn't understand her homework.

7:22 P.M.: While looking for the dishwashing soap, I discover my son under the sink playing Johnny Space Commander. I ask him if he has finished his homework, but he tells me he only speaks Tironi and would I please close his space capsule—he can't breathe.

7:23 P.M.: I walk by the linen closet and shout: "The kids are asleep!" Inside the closet, a little voice retorts: "Liar!"

7:30 P.M.: After much fanfare that includes bringing 3,154 little green army men into the bathtub, my son climbs into the water with both of his socks on.

7:42 P.M.: From upstairs, I hear the distant sound of my daughter crying that her homework still isn't finished, and if her parents really cared, they would help her with it. To which I answer in reply, "Honey, will you go get me a towel from the linen closet?"

7:45 P.M.: Choosing not to towel off first, my son leaves the bathroom and walks to his bedroom, where he puts his pajamas on his wet body. By the time I find him, he's squirming on the floor in his soaked jammies with his arms pulled behind his back and his head stuck in the collar. Meanwhile, I'm standing in a puddle of water in my socks.

7:46 P.M.: My wife passes by and exclaims: "Traitor!"

8 P.M.: By the grace of God, both children are in bed.

8:03 P.M.: My son builds a blanket fort stretching from his bedroom to his sister's bedroom complete with plastic wrap windows. I notice that in the fort he has created, my pillow is the dog's bed.

9:30 P.M.: The kids finally fall asleep.

9:31 P.M.: I go to bed—dreaming of all those things I'll do one day when the children fall asleep on time.

I just hope I remember what those things are by the time the kids get married and move away.

Being a father does have its advantages though . . . at least, that's what my wife keeps saying. Actually, she says I've got it better than her—but that might not be saying much.

I do enjoy, however, being there to guide my children—to help them conquer their fears. Like the time when my son was ready to defeat our town's number one nemesis: the state fair's roller coaster, affectionately called "Killer." Unfortunately, he took one look at the mighty beast and started to cry. He left the fair feeling defeated.

He made a pledge before God and his family: "The next time will be different," he exclaimed. He said he'd ride Killer like a true bronco buster.

I prepared my son for the big day. We talked excitedly about his first ride. I'd even occasionally drive by the mighty roller coaster so he could stare it down.

"That's the one you're going to ride, right?" I'd ask him as if warning Killer of his impending doom.

"That's right!" my son would shout.

As the days grew closer, my son was even more adamant that he would make the daring ride. He drew pictures of the roller coaster. At dinner he sculpted its deep, sloped tracks in his mashed potatoes. He named his pet frog Killer.

You would think that when we walked into the state fair and he saw the infamous ride, he'd start jumping up for joy, wouldn't you? Instead, his eyes got real wide and he vomited.

"Honey, are you okay?" his mom asked him. "You don't have to go on the roller coaster if you don't want to do it."

"It's called Killer and he's fine," I argued, taking my boy by the hand. "He just ate a bad corn dog. Isn't that right, son?"

His white, ashen face bobbled nervously.

"Ken, leave him alone," my wife interjected. "He said he didn't want to go on it!"

"No, he didn't," I argued. "He threw up on his shoes and now he's collecting his thoughts."

"Ken, it looks to me like he changed his mind."

"That's just excitement," I explained.

"Then why do you have him in a fireman's carry?"

As I put my son down, he exclaimed, "Dad, I'm too scared—I . . . I don't want to do it."

I told him not to be silly as I drew his attention to a three-year-old girl getting off the ride. "If she can do it, you can."

"Ken, they stopped it to let her off," my wife interrupted.

"Only because she was screaming too loud," I countered. "She loved it. Look, she's trying to wiggle out of her dad's arms so she can get back on the roller coaster."

"She's convulsing."

I took my wife aside. "Honey," I whispered, "this is for our son's benefit. As his dad, I have to prepare him to face his fears. You know, so he's ready for the everyday demands of the adult world."

"How are our days like a roller coaster?" she asked. "It's not like I've seen you moving down the McDonald's drive-thru with your arms over your head screaming like an idiot."

Later, on our way home from the fair, I turned my head to the backseat of the car and looked at my son. "Next year you're going to ride Killer, right?"

He nodded his head.

"Cool," I exclaimed.

We both knew he was lying.

Killer reminds me a lot of the excitement dads get during spring training . . . Little League, that is.

I've seen the highs and lows of baseball fever.

Last April, one of the guys in the neighborhood mentioned the upcoming baseball season, and we realized that our kids would be playing each other in the same Little League. Soon, my neighbors began bragging about their kids and bantering around some challenges.

I felt my stomach pitch (no pun intended) when I heard this. Last year, in T-ball, my son was less-than-athletically enthused. Don't get me wrong, he's coordinated. But typically, when the other kids were paying attention to the baseball game, my son was throwing grass up in the air and trying to catch it in his mouth.

During the practice season, I decided I wouldn't put the pressure on my son or myself this year by trying to raise a super baseball player at home. And I wouldn't engage in the bragging and one-upmanships on the street.

Then, when I arrived for the first game, I saw John Miller giving his son last-minute pointers. Suddenly, in a moment of insecurity, I, too, turned to my boy and whispered some game-playing advice: "Son, watch out for doggie doo-doo on the grass."

During the seventh inning, John wandered over to our side and shook my hand.

"Great game, huh?" he said.

I nodded.

"Too bad about your son falling down on his way to third base, though," he continued. "Is he alright?"

"He's okay," I explained, my face turning red. "His stomach is bothering him—he had a big dinner."

"Really? I thought maybe he accidentally ate a rotten weed or some bad thatch."

I knew word of that would spread through the neighborhood quickly.

"I don't want to go outside anymore," I told my wife.

"If you really want to do something," she said, "you should take Alasdair out to the park this weekend and practice."

I felt bad for expecting more from my son than he wished to give, but I took her advice nonetheless. I grabbed my son's hand and we walked around the infield. I pointed out the excitement of the game. We talked about each position. I explained how grass would give him worms.

For the next several weeks, my son actually showed an interest in the game.

Once, he even caught the game-ending fly ball. As I stood and watched his teammates congratulate him, I silently patted myself on the back for encouraging him to try harder.

The next day, I even joined in the banter around the mailbox. It was fun bragging about my kid's final out. I had reached the inner circle. I felt a part of something greater than myself.

High on the moment, I even predicted that my son's team would "whoop" the team John's kid was on later that evening.

At the ballpark, I walked confidently over to John on the bleachers.

"Great game," I remarked.

"You bet," he replied.

"Yep, I think we are going to win this one," I boasted, just as a fly ball landed two feet behind my son, who, at that moment, was hunched over on the grass spitting on a ladybug.

"See you around the neighborhood," John exclaimed as he rushed down to congratulate his son for hitting the game-winning home run.

My glory days as a sports dad were short-lived, but I'll always remember them fondly. *(Sigh)*

After an experience like that, I'm still surprised by what I did next. In my defense, though, I momentarily lost thought control, and the next thing I knew, I was loading golf clubs into my car while my wife was asking me where I was going with our son.

"I'm taking him golfing."

Her eyes narrowed. "Since when?"

"Since now," I answered. "He's old enough."

She stood looking at me for a couple seconds. "Is this a Tiger Woods thing?"

"Huh?"

"Gloria down the street said her husband takes little Jimmy to the driving range every weekend hoping to produce the next Tiger Woods. Is that what you are doing?"

I shrugged.

"You aren't going to change his name to Grizzly or Leopard, you know," she announced.

"I know," I answered, rolling my eyes. "He wants Kodiak."

"No I don't," my son interrupted, poking his head out the car window. "Flamingo."

"Flamingo Swarner?"

"We're going to be famous," I yelled out the window as I drove away.

Several hours later, we returned. As we drove up, my wife walked out to the car. "How did it go?" she asked with an impish grin.

"Okay," I replied.

She turned to my son. "Flamingo, did you hit the golf ball?"

"Yep," he answered. "I accidentally hit Daddy, too."

I nodded. "I made the assumption he'd swing after I was done teeing up his ball."

"I hit him with an 8 club."

"Wow, you already know the names of your clubs?" she asked.

"Not really," he said, pointing at my face. "I can still see the number imprinted on Daddy's forehead."

I climbed out of the car.

"Are you limping?" she asked me.

"Don't ask."

"Did you replace all your divots like a good boy?" she asked him.

"No—the golf course guy said we didn't have to."

She looked at me.

I grimaced. "We're taking grass seed and topsoil over tomorrow."

My son's face brightened. "I get to stomp it down!"

We walked inside and unloaded our equipment.

"Flamingo, did you do anything else exciting?"

"I wrote my name!" he said proudly.

"On a scorecard with one of these little pencils?" she asked.

"No," he replied. "In the sand trap with a rake."

I sat down on the couch. "That was right after he jammed a Hot Wheel in the ball washer. Some guy in the twosome behind us threw his back out trying to unwedge it."

My wife sat down next to me. "So, Flamingo Swarner is on his way to the Masters, huh?"

"Yep," my son retorted, running outside to play.

"Do you now realize how silly this whole golf thing was?" she asked me.

"Yes," I replied. "I was just thinking how far off base I was."

She nodded.

We sat quietly for a few moments, then I broke the silence: "What age do you suppose Pete Sampras started playing tennis?"

"Probably when his dad tore down the garage and built a tennis court in the driveway."

I stared at her. "You know, that might work."

She left the room.

I shouted after her. "He's going to be a tennis star! You'll see!"

Speaking of seeing things, I used to see my kids. There was a time they couldn't wait for me to get home from work. The moment I put my briefcase down they'd climb up on my lap and recount their day at school or what happened on the playground.

Lately, however, I've been lucky to see them at all, let alone receive two complete sentences at the dinner table before they gulp their milk and rush back outside to play.

I guess I thought they'd always be underfoot—screaming in my ear, kneeing my groin, and head-butting me when I wasn't looking. But, just when I settled into this comfortable pattern of parenting, my children have passed on to a new, invisible stage of development.

That's why I complained as I walked into my house the other day after work. "I don't believe it!"

"What?" my wife asked.

"The kids didn't even wave as I drove up—they just kept on playing with those neighbor kids."

"So?"

"So," I said, "remember when our children used to have their little faces plastered to the front window waiting for me to get home?"

"Actually, I think they were looking for the ice-cream man."

"And as I drove up, they'd come running out of the house."

"I was chasing them with a broom."

"See what I mean?"

"No, I don't," my wife answered.

"I'm yesterday's piggyback ride," I explained, walking over to the window to watch the kids playing outside. "A dad replaced by kick-the-can and new friends."

My wife joined me. "Ken, the kids are still young—you're acting as if they are teenagers already."

"No, I'm not!" I stammered. "Teenagers wave."

"Yeah, when you're leaving and they have a hundred friends coming over to party on your coffee table."

She obviously didn't understand, and I was about to skulk out of the room, when she said, "I thought this is what you wanted?"

I wheeled around. "I didn't ask to be abandoned by my own children."

"Yes you did," she continued. "Just three months ago you looked toward the heavens and screamed, 'God, give my kids a hobby!'"

"That's because they locked me out of the house."

She shook her head.

"I was wearing your fuzzy raccoon slippers."

Leading me over to the couch, she said, "Ken, why don't you enjoy the peace and quiet? Think back on all those times you wished the kids would go play on their own—this is your chance to do the things you want to do."

"I can't," I moaned.

"Why, because your feelings are hurt?"

"No."

"Because you feel guilty?"

"No."

She stood looking at me for a couple minutes. "Oh, I see," she finally said. "You've been a parent so long, you can't remember what you liked to do."

My face fell into my hands. "Do you think if I agree to be 'it,' the kids will let me play kick-the-can with them?"

My wife wasn't too worried about any of that, but I should tell you that she has this fear of death.

Not the dying part—she can handle that. Rather, she's afraid to leave me in sole charge of the children.

It's not their safety she's concerned about. It's the little things.

"If I die, will you let our daughter wear white patent leather shoes at Christmastime?" she asked me one day.

"What does that have to do with anything?"

"Look how you dressed your daughter," she said pointing to my darling child.

"What?!"

"Those ruffles on her outfit."

"Yeah? They're cute."

"They go on her behind, not her stomach."

They looked fine to me.

"Honestly, Ken! What will you do when I'm gone?"

I blinked. "I doubt my seven-year-old daughter will need help with her Elmo socks."

"I could leave tomorrow and the next day my daughter will be wearing red pants with pink shoes and a ponytail fastened with a bread clip."

"One time and I'm labeled for life!"

"Forgetting her underwear?"

"Two times!"

"The thongs in January?"

"You can't blame that on me. The school never sent a memo."

She frowned. "Your idea of an outfit, Ken, is whatever can be thrown on the fastest. I'm surprised you don't slip a trash bag over their heads and be done with it."

"They trip up in the plastic and sandwich bags are too small."

"What are you going to do when I'm gone?" my wife moaned.

"We'll have new priorities," I answered. "They'll wear the kinds of clothes I like."

"Red shirts and purple shorts?"

"Is that bad?"

"Yes!"

I sat quietly for a moment. "It's not like we are the First Family. I seriously doubt we'll make *People* magazine's worst-dressed list. Why is this clothing stuff so important to you?"

"Because, the PTA is still talking about the holiday concert when I was in New York."

"The music teacher said the girls had to wear a long, white dress," I argued.

"You put our daughter in my slip."

"It matched her shoes."

Her face fell into her hands. "Pray I outlive you."

"Honey, if it makes you feel any better," I said, "when you are gone, I'll marry someone who's even better than you in taking care of children."

"Don't you dare!" she yelled and stormed out of the room.

I don't get it . . . would someone please explain to me what's wrong with white shoes at Christmas?

6

Let's Go Crazy

"They rushed to meet the insulting foe;
they took the spear—but left the shield."

—Philip Freneau

My wife and I have been completely overwhelmed by parenting.

I don't mean overwhelmed in the Kodak moment sense—the times your breath is literally taken away by watching your children grow and interact with the world and you are in awe of the whole experience.

Instead, I am referring to those moments when I'm ten minutes late to work and I wonder if I'll get a call from the principal if she sees my child jumping from my car at two miles per hour.

Is it just me, or are there other parents who feel someone is turning every clock in their world forward indiscriminately throughout the day when nobody is looking?

I can never get it together. I am always five minutes behind, even when I wake up two hours early.

So to survive my world, I've become a rusher. So has my wife. We're rushers.

Our kids get the worst of it.

"Alright children, get into bed."

"We haven't had dinner!"

"Don't panic, Mom has the pit stop open on the stairs— yum, its liquid steak and peas night. Drink fast. And, by the way, sleep in tomorrow's school clothes so we're ready to go early —THE NICE ONES, you have class pictures."

Of course, the trouble with kids is that you can't success- fully rush them. And once they know you're a rusher, they'll use it against you.

"Kids, Daddy is going to be late for work if we don't leave right now!" I shouted recently.

"I can't find my jacket," my daughter explained.

"Did you check the mailbox?"

"Yes," she said rolling her eyes.

"How about your closet?" I asked.

"Huh?" She paused. "I'll go check."

Meanwhile I was pacing . . . I was worrying . . . I was telling the cat about the billion things that I had to do that day. (Cats don't care.)

"It's not here," she finally called.

"Well, wear your bathrobe."

"What?"

"Sure, kids do it all the time," I explained. "WE HAVE TO GO!"

"No. I'm not budging until you find my jacket."

I ran into her room and rummaged through her closet. "Al- right, I'll give you a dollar if you wear this."

"My Halloween costume?"

"It's fleece," I said.

"It's Peter Cottontail, Dad."

"Just tuck the ears in the hat and I'll drop you off at the back of the school."

Of course my daughter's principal called and wanted to discuss why the Easter Bunny jumped out of my moving car that morning.

I told her it had a lot to do with how the morning began. It started when I jolted up to the sound of my wife's clamorous shriek: "We're late!"

I looked at her as if a mushroom cloud was blooming outside in the distance. "Again?!" It was the fifteenth time that month. I jumped out of bed and hurried to the bathroom.

"Wait," my wife said, calling me back into the bedroom. "Do I look like I just got up?"

"You did just get up," I answered.

"I know, but does my hair look like it?" she asked.

"Well . . ."

"It's just that I don't have much time, so do you think I need to take a shower?"

"You don't have to," I answered.

She smiled. "That's a relief."

"Yeah," I continued, "you can just tell people that on your way to work this morning you fell down in the parking lot."

She jumped in the shower as my son walked in rubbing the sleep out of his eyes. "I forgot to do my homework last night and I need help," he said. He was followed by my daughter, who announced: "I need a can for a school art project today."

They both also informed me that they were out of clean underwear.

I think the frenzied look on my face gave them pause.

"It's every poor Swarner for himself, this morning," I said shaking my head.

I turned around to grab a towel as my wife stopped in front of me.

"Can you see the run in my stocking?" she asked, her eyes pleading for a "No."

"The one that looks like the Panama Canal?" I answered matter-of-factly, "or Lake Michigan by your knee?"

"Dang!" she said—quickly pulling the tights off her legs. "I guess I'll forget the skirt!" She started throwing clothes out of her drawer. "Is this going to be our kids' memories of growing up?" she asked, grabbing her pants. "Their parents running frantically around trying to get to work on time?"

"I doubt it," I answered. "I think they'll mostly remember the times they drank their cereal from a thermos in the back-seat of my car as I've sped to school."

The panty hose conversation left me 30 seconds to shower. As I hastily toweled off, my son shouted down the hall. "Dad, how do you spell 'balancing'?!"

"I'm not dressed!" I yelled.

"You have to be wearing clothes to spell 'balancing'?!"

"No, I could forget about getting dressed this morning, come into your room, and spell 'balancing,'" I replied. "And then, later, I can also spell my name for the nice police officer after being arrested for driving on the roads in nothing but a ratty bath towel."

"You can get arrested for that?"

"That, and traumatizing a busload of schoolchildren."

After I managed to get dressed, I had time to zip up the back of my daughter's Peter Cottontail outfit. I grabbed a handful of Grape-Nuts and shepherded both children into the car.

"Don't spill that cereal!" I shouted as I closed their doors.

As my wife climbed into her own car to leave, she paused

to check her watch. "Twenty-two minutes to get ready this morning."

"Not bad," I exclaimed, getting into my seat. "I never thought we'd break twenty-five this year."

"Maybe we should check and see if Guinness has an award for this."

I shook my head and closed the door.

I'd just settle for some Dramamine.

That was an easy morning because the kids bought lunch that day. Things really bog down, though, when I have to make school lunches in the middle-of-the morning fire drill.

I was looking through one of those parenting magazines and noticed an interesting article on creative school lunches. There were step-by-step directions on how to build triple-decker towers with lunch meat and personal pan pizzas that fit in a lunchbox. All the time I was looking at the pictures, I kept thinking, *Are these people insane? They should do a series of my recipes for the frantic parent called "Whatever's Quickest."*

I am really good at rushing around the house in a perpetual state of being late, grabbing anything that looks edible and spreading peanut butter on it.

Of course, my kids are less than impressed.

"Dad!" my daughter shrieked from the backseat of the car as we drove to school one day.

"What?" I asked.

"You can't put peanut butter on leftover noodles," she complained, pointing at her lunchbox.

"It's good."

"It's embarrassing," she added.

"For who?"

"Me," she explained. "Kids make fun of my lunches."

"They do? What do they say?"

"'Gross!'"

I frowned. "What do you say back?"

"I lie. I tell them you're a famous chef and my lunches are works of art."

My son nodded. "I tell everyone you're autistic."

I shook my head.

Then my son looked in his lunchbox.

"I'm not eating this," he said.

"What's wrong with melba toast?" I asked.

"You put pepper jelly on them."

"So? It was leftover from your mother's bridge group."

"Couldn't I have had tuna fish?" he replied.

"No, I didn't have time. It takes too long to open the can."

"I'm going to have to change schools," my son complained.

"Your friends don't approve of melba toast?"

"No, it's just that there's a lot of violence in the schools to-day. And this," he said, pointing to the sandwich, "is going to make a lot of people angry."

I was silent for a few moments. "So what you are telling me is, you don't think you'll ever see one of my creations in a magazine?"

"Not unless it's a story on bizarre tribal customs," my son exclaimed.

"Or it could be one of those 'before' pictures in a before and after article," my daughter added.

Later that night, when I got home, I went into my den and tore up the query letter and sample recipes I had addressed to *Good Housekeeping*.

Of course, my kids said my idea for a *Quick Bites for Dinner* cookbook is hopeless as well.

I thought it would be helpful because I've never found a good cookbook for a family on the go. Let's be honest. Who has time anymore to preplan a meal with a conventional cookbook? That requires leafing through the recipes, writing out a shopping list, not losing the list before arriving at the store, finding what you're looking for (like anise), then cooking the meal before the children have eaten the ingredients.

When it's my turn to cook dinner, I usually plan it five minutes before it's time to eat with whatever is available.

Therefore, I've proposed a cookbook that works backward and is based on ingredients, not the final product. For example, if you rushed home from work and all you had was leftover turkey, a can of cream soup, and a brick of cheese with a bite out of it, you could look up those ingredients and my book would match up turkey divan. But if you had lamb, Raisin Bran, and salsa, my book would suggest foraging outside for roots and berries.

No one has published my idea, so only my family has reaped the benefits of these recipes . . . and that's when they run screaming into the laundry chute: "No, not the chicken waffles again!"

"Critics. Write your own book!"

Recently, I was finally instructed (threatened) by my family to buy a conventional cookbook . . . any cookbook.

"Recipes don't work for me," I told my wife. "I'm much better at throwing in a little of this, a pinch of that, and blending it all together."

"Same way you dress the kids?"

"Okay, pink and red don't match."

"Neither does this meat and chocolate-chip loaf," she said looking at her plate.

"I don't have time to organize dinner," I complained.

"But you had time to create this, Dr. Frankenstein?"

"If you don't want to eat it . . . don't!"

"Eat it?" she said. "I was thinking about making up the guest room for it."

My daughter's eyes brightened. "Can it sleep in my room tonight, Daddy?"

"That's it!" I shouted.

"Where are you going?"

"To buy some cookbooks!" I yelled. "I'm getting *Liver, Liver, Liver* and *The Joy of Lima Beans*."

Of course, there isn't much need for too many cookbooks in our house, considering our lifestyle.

People sometimes will look at my seemingly well-put-together family and ask how two busy parents manage to get it all done without any bloodshed.

Sometimes, I lie, and tell them that it is because I am a well-organized, natural leader. But most of the time, I just admit that I owe it all to take-out.

Take-out has seen me through all of those hectic, running-around-like-a-chicken-with-my-head-cut-off moments. It has been there for those early evening soccer practices and ballet lessons. It has been there for PTA, Brownies, Bingo Night, and the time my daughter broke her collarbone on the swing set.

Like a lighthouse during a raging storm, or a St. Bernard with a jug of brandy in the middle of a blizzard, take-out has been a godsend.

Incidentally, I have met people who have never done take-out for dinner, but instead, for years, have cooked their meals at home. I can only assume one of three things about them:

1. They have time to prepare casseroles on the weekend and freeze them.

2. They eat a lot of health food (no take-out for that).

3. They're weird.

Of course, there was a week that I, too, didn't stop for food on the way home. A few years back, I had come to the conclusion that take-out cost a fortune, was making me fat, and freaked out my son when he couldn't find Pizza Hut on the food pyramid. So for four, long, miserable days, my wife and I challenged us to eat a home-cooked meal every night. It was an interesting experiment.

On Monday, we were late signing escrow with the Realtor after work, so by the time we got home, the kids had a half-hour to eat before bed. I think my wife summed it up best when she said: "Ice cream, anyone?"

On Tuesday, my wife called me at work and asked: "Ken, did you remember to take anything out of the freezer this morning for dinner?"

My eyes twitched. "I was going to," I replied, "but just before I could, the cat got tangled up in the phone cord, the Salvation Army knocked at the door, your son answered the door without any clothes on, and your daughter was screaming that someone threw her hair clip in the toilet."

On Wednesday, I anticipated a problem because my wife and I had a PTA meeting right after work, followed by the family Cub Scout presentation: Know your tourniquet. So that morning, I packed a picnic dinner, but, as I drove around all day, the food rolled out onto the backseat. Later, when my wife opened the door to get it, Waldorf salad fell on her shoe.

On Thursday, everything went haywire, and the kids were clamoring for take-out. My wife and I, however, never formally told the children about our new take-out policy (we didn't want to frighten them), so as I drove past our normal haunts without stopping, they demanded an answer. I told the kids it was a day of fasting in our church. That worked well until they saw our church choir director coming out of Burger King with several bags in her hands. Still, I think I covered nicely when I rolled down my window and screamed "Satan!" at her.

Needless to say, by that Friday, my wife and I came to our senses and returned to our take-out lifestyle.

We felt much better.

We still, however, don't feel better about day care pick-up time.

There has been a lot of discussion about the cause and effect of road rage, but, if you ask me, the whole afternoon rush hour would be much safer if day cares were open longer.

The real wackos on the highways are working parents like me trying desperately to reach our children before closing time at 6 P.M.

Day cares are very particular about their policies. When I signed up my son, they handed me an inch-thick packet of rules that included, among many things, a large-print section that stated the center closes at 6 P.M. Very few people actually know what happens if you aren't there by 6 P.M., but I figured that it must be bad.

So, it is easily understood why, when I was running behind the other day, and I found myself in thick rush-hour traffic, the only recourse I had, was to scream: "I'M LATE!!!"

Suddenly, desperate, horrible thoughts raced through my head. I imagined driving up to the day care to find the owner, a couple cops, Child Protective Services, and an elderly neighbor all standing in the darkened driveway waiting to arrest me for child abandonment.

That's when the wrong person cut me off on the freeway.

My first reaction was similar to how an Indy 500 racer probably feels when pushed up against the wall at 150 miles per hour: I wanted to wrap my steering wheel around the other driver's face.

Then, after I had calmed down, I pulled around the car, screaming at the top of my lungs like an attacking Calvary leader: "I've got to get my sonnnnnnnn!"

Once alongside the offending car, I rolled down my window and shouted directly at the startled driver: "Thank you! Thank you very much! Maybe my son will get a nice meal at the foster home!"

Finally, I cut narrowly back in front of the aggressive driver flashing a particular kind of sign language that they don't teach at my child's day care . . . and I sped off down the highway.

Hopefully I can find a day care that is open later before I roll down my window on the road and accidentally yell at someone I know.

The voice mails of Christmas:

(Husband's voice mail)
8:30 A.M.:
Hi Ken. I forgot to remind you to buy a fruitcake for the neighborhood party tomorrow night. I'll see you tonight at the school concert. Is it just me, or has this holiday season seemed a lot less stressful than last year? Just call me Suzy Snowflake. Bye.

(Wife's voice mail)

9:02 A.M.:

I remembered the fruitcake. I even bought a red bow. See ya
at 6.

(Husband's voice mail)

10:30 A.M.:

Hi, I stopped to pick up Claire's concert dress at the dry
cleaners and it's not ready—even though it was supposed to
be. Sorry, but can you pick Alasdair up at school today and
get him to swimming lessons? That way I have time to get
the dress before taking Claire to gymnastics. Grab some
dinner, and then meet me at 6 P.M. in the school parking lot.
I'm off to pick your sister up at the airport. Fa la la la—la la
la—la-la-la— I am putting on a happy face.

(Wife's voice mail)

10:55 A.M.:

Swimming lessons—got it. By the way, I was supposed to
bring something to my office holiday party today and I forgot. So I've commandeered the fruitcake. Maybe we could
give the neighbors the venison your dad gave us. I saved the
red bow.

(Husband's voice mail)

12:45 P.M.:

Ken, where are you? Your sister didn't get off the plane. At
this point, I am going to assume one of two things: 1. She
has been kidnapped and Christmas is ruined. Or, 2. She has
been waiting for hours at a different gate, and as I speak, is
stuffing our Christmas gifts in a trash bin. This little irritat-
ing incident has me behind schedule, so you have to stop at

the dry cleaners and pick up Claire's dress while I am at gymnastics. Remember, if you forget the dress, your daughter will be the only third-grader in the school concert wearing a tumbling outfit.

(Wife's voice mail)
2:55 P.M.:
Allison, I just picked your son up at school. Did you know he needed cotton balls for an art project tomorrow? I just stopped at the store, but they were out, so I bought Q-tips. Did you find my sister?

(Husband's voice mail)
3:15 P.M.:
Your sister isn't coming in until tomorrow—she changed her mind and forgot to tell us. Guess who gets the venison? I'll look for cotton balls when I buy 24 cupcakes, juice, and candy for your daughter's school party tomorrow, which I JUST found out about TODAY. Apparently, I am the only parent in that class not trapped under something heavy this holiday season. I'm off to gymnastics. Pray for me.

(Wife's voice mail)
5:35 P.M.:
Don't panic if I'm not there exactly at 6—I am running behind schedule because the swim class did a special holiday handstand in the shallow end for the parents. Your son got water up his nose. If he tells you we ate ice cream for dinner, ignore him. I'm going to pick up the dress now.

(Husband's voice mail)
6:10 P.M.:

Why aren't you here?! Claire's class does Rudolph the Red-Nose Reindeer in 20 minutes. I'll run inside and see if I can stall. Now I know how the Grinch feels!

(Wife's voice mail)
6:16 P.M.:
Suzy Snowflake, don't freak out when you hear this, but the dry cleaners can't find the dress—so I've been thinking about the tumbling outfit. Maybe the choir director could have Claire do a back handspring when Rudolph goes down in history.

(In person)
6:22 P.M.:
%!#

7

Serving Two Masters

> ""Work! Work! Work!"
> —Thomas Hood

Are your children affecting your work?

Were you recently passed over for that raise? Do your co-workers snicker behind your back? Do you have the sneaking suspicion that your role as parent may be affecting your advancement at work? Before you read any farther in this book, it's best to see where you stand in the job world. The following test was created in my lab to ferret out a person's employment status. As you follow along, keep track of your A, B, and C answers.

1. **The Daily Grind.** Getting the proper amount of sleep at night is one of the major contributing factors to workplace performance. For parents, that can be a sticky issue. How do you feel at work?

   A. I am energized from morning to night, and in fact, I find that working on the weekend boosts my stamina.

B. Sometimes, after lunch, I feel a little tired, but that goes away by mid-afternoon.

C. The only way I can stay awake during a staff meeting is by holding a permanent marker to my nose.

2. **Communications.** We usually spend some time on the phone making personal calls. If your co-workers were polled, how would they describe your typical personal phone conversation?

A. "Sorry, I'm going to have to cancel our date. I have to work late tonight."

B. "Hi honey. Did you remember to pick up my tux at the dry cleaners?"

C. "What?! Well, reach your hand in the toilet and fish it out!"

3. **Conversations.** There are so many things we can say to our co-workers. What's your standard line?

A. "Your presentation was terrific. I bet you can count on a big raise this year."

B. "Wow! That outfit looks great on you. Is it new?"

C. "Hi. Would you like to buy some Girl Scout cookies?"

4. **Accessories.** Keeping up on fashions in the workplace can be a struggle for many—but more so for parents. How would you describe your ensemble today?

A. Designer business suit with complementary scarf and shoes.

B. Conservative ensemble with well-polished shoes.

C. Outdated dress with a dried macaroni necklace as the only accessory.

5. **Performance.** We are often rated on how we excel above and beyond the call of duty. For each person, there is a different measurement for this. How do you give your all to work?

   A. Every week, I exceed my previous week's performance goals, plus, I wash the president's car.

   B. I am the first to volunteer for special projects at work.

   C. Once, I stayed an extra five minutes after closing time (but only because soccer practice started late that day).

6. **Awards and Accolades.** Being recognized for a job well done actually ranks above pay in worker satisfaction surveys. How have you been recognized at work lately?

   A. At the annual meeting, I was named Employee of the Year.

   B. At a recent staff meeting, I was congratulated for perfect attendance.

   C. At the corporate picnic, I was voted most likely to smell like baby wipes.

7. **Lessons Learned.** High school and college aren't the only places we learn new things in this world. 20/20 hindsight teaches us many things about working

with other adults. What's a key thing you've learned recently while operating in a group environment?

A. Everyone likes his or her voice to be heard.

B. Groups work best when there is a shared vision and commitment.

C. Nothing breaks up a watercooler discussion faster than someone mentioning nipple confusion.

8. **Personal Business.** How many times have you left work recently to attend to personal business? Parents surely know what it means to get time off for school concerts and children's dentist appointments. How we ask for time off directly reflects the number of times we make these requests. How do you approach your supervisors?

A. I never take time off. Ever!

B. I work a lot of extra hours, so it is easy to ask for time off when I need to leave the office on personal business.

C. I leave so often, I have to devise diversions. The last time, I grabbed a little packet of ketchup from my top desk drawer, squirted it in my eyes, and ran screaming out of the building.

9. **Sharing the Wealth.** The workplace is an outstanding place for employees to bring things from home. It's not uncommon to walk in the staff room and find little treats from a co-worker, or to have a co-

worker make crafts and pass them around the office. What have you brought to work lately?

A. I brought imported Belgian chocolates with liqueur inside for everyone to enjoy.

B. I made holiday lapel pins for the ladies on my staff.

C. I gave the entire office my son's vomiting virus.

Your Score

Now, tally up your scores. Give yourself 10 points for every A answer, 5 points for every B answer, and 1 point for a C response.

If you scored 75 points or more, you can probably expect a big, fat raise in your mailbox any day now.

If you scored more than 50 points, you are what employers consider "irreplaceable."

If your score was more than 25 points, don't despair—you only have 30 more years until retirement.

If your score was below 24 points, isn't it about time you looked for a new job?

I have been enjoying my job a whole lot more now that Larry Johnson packed his belongings and moved out of our department.

I don't want to appear insensitive, but, you can't have someone with that much free time and a calm disposition dragging down you or your co-workers.

For years, my associates and I attended to our jobs just fine and we all planned to stay there until we retired.

Then, last December, Larry arrived. I took one look at him and called an emergency meeting in the break room.

"I don't want to panic anyone," I said, "but there's something peculiar about the new guy."

The staff looked concerned.

"Did anyone notice his clothes? They're pressed."

A wave of fear spread across their faces.

"His complexion is clear. His hair is combed. His shoes are shined."

People started to weep.

"You mean to tell us . . ." Steve from Purchasing started to say.

"Yes," I interrupted. "I don't think he has kids."

Everyone screamed.

We sent a reconnaissance squad to Larry's desk to confirm my suspicions.

"Sure enough," the squad leader reported back, "but it's worse than you thought. He's not even married."

The problems started immediately. While we were doing what we always did: shuttling kids to doctor's appointments, rushing home for forgotten school lunches, and hawking Boy Scout fund-raisers in the elevator, Larry was working late, arriving early, and eating his dinner at his desk.

Then, the inevitable happened—the boss noticed.

"Has anyone seen how hard Larry is working?" he barked.

How could we tell our leader from the *Leave It to Beaver* generation that we had responsibilities to our children? He'd never understand. Out of fear for our jobs, we tried to keep up. Many of us worked 10 or 15 minutes past quitting time. I even skipped my son's pre-season soccer tournament to complete a major project over the weekend, but that backfired when my supervisor caught me in the men's bathroom listening to my wife's play-by-play of the game over my cell phone. Even Gloria Freeman, the pillar of strength in Accounting, couldn't handle the pressure. She transferred out of our department to the night shift. She has three kids in competitive ice skating . . . who could blame her?

Finally, I had to lay it on the line with the boss: "Maybe Larry would be a good candidate for that new job in Department Six," I suggested to him. "You'd look good, sir, for recommending him."

That's how we got rid of Larry "No Kids" Johnson.

The next day, Larry's replacement showed up with a hint of baby formula behind each ear and a paperclip necklace as her only accessory.

I was the first to greet her. "So, do you plan to work overtime here?" I asked nervously.

She winced. "Do you see these dark circles around my eyes? I was up at the crack of dawn digging a pacifier out of the compost pile, and when I leave here, I have to drive ten giggly Brownies clear across town to the slaughterhouse so they can earn their farming badge. Who has time to work?"

She has my vote for employee of the year.

I'd have to say that working and parenting are like juggling apples and chain saws. It literally takes a magician to coordinate everyone's schedules so that when evening finally falls, the children are all picked up from their activities, fund-raisers are sold, dinner is served, and you're still invited back the next day to earn a paycheck.

To do this, it takes a lot of patience, a little aspirin, and a daytimer with lots of space. Of course, life as I knew it ended precisely at 9:07 A.M., Monday, February 21. It was the exact moment I realized that I had lost my Day-Timer.

For those of you who understand the magnitude of this tragedy, I assume your hands are sweating at just the thought of it.

I remember walking around my office in a daze. "I'm doomed," I told a co-worker. "The atom bomb might as well come—what kind of life can I have now?"

"Don't be ridiculous," he laughed. "Certainly, you know what appointments you had today?"

I nodded. "For work, yes."

"Then what's wrong?"

"I'm supposed to be at my daughter's day care this afternoon for the annual Preschool Cooking Festival, but I can't remember what time it starts."

I paused for my friend's acknowledgment that yes, my life IS spinning violently out of control, but instead, he just stared blankly. "I have to be there," I continued matter-of-factly. "I'm in charge of making sure the toddlers don't lick the mixing spoons. If I'm late, they'll have to move Janet Penshaw from carrots and dip into my spot, and then no one will be there to stop the double-dipping!"

"I'm sure missing one thing won't be a big deal," my friend retorted.

"But, that's only the half of it," I explained. "I can't remember what else was in my daytimer for today. Is this the day I'm supposed to meet my wife after work to sign escrow papers? Or maybe, I was supposed to pick up my daughter at her ballet class. And what if I'm late picking up my son at soccer practice because I can't remember what time it's over? He has an active imagination—he'll probably think I'm dead."

"I'm sure the coach would wait with him and tell your son not to worry."

"I'm sure he would," I agreed, "and, that would be somewhat of a comfort to my sobbing son. Of course, from here on out, I'll never be able to say the word *soccer* again without my son wetting his pants."

My friend started rummaging around my desk, looking for the Day-Timer.

I slumped into my chair. "There's no room for error, here," I explained, mostly to myself. "My wife and I have a finely crafted schedule that would make Federal Express envious. But it is all dependent on split-second action and precise movements. If I don't find my Day-Timer, I could have family members all over town in a state of confusion. Then, there I'll be, on the 6 o'clock news tonight, showing a picture of my wife and kids, pleading for someone to find them and bring them home to Daddy."

I was about to continue when the boss walked around the corner, holding my Day-Timer. I felt my spirits lift like a soaring eagle.

"Whose Day-Timer is this?" the boss asked, holding it up.

I was about to reach for it when he continued. "I thought I might recognize who this belongs to," he continued, "but I can't find any references in this calendar to the work we do here."

I froze.

He plopped the book down hard on the table and walked away as everyone looked around, waiting for the owner to present himself.

I decided to sneak it off the table later, when no one was looking. In the meantime, all I could do was hope that my daughter wasn't double-dipping the carrots.

As would be expected, eventually, my boss DID catch on to my active family schedule, as evidenced by a recent exchange of e-mails between him and myself:

11:01 A.M.:
Dear Ken,
I stopped by your cubicle this morning and you weren't

there. I noticed your Day-Timer said 10 A.M. meeting with
Arts and Crafts committee. Is that a new client of ours?
Who's Art, and who's Craft? It's now 11 A.M. and there's no
sign of you. At noon, I'll file a missing person's report. I
hope you're not locked in the executive washroom.
Your boss,
Jerry

11:32 A.M.:
Dear Jerry,
I guess I just missed you. No, Arts and Crafts was an emergency Cub Scout training session for this weekend's Jam-
boree. (We learned how to make pencil holders out of soup
cans and string. I'd like you to have mine.) Believe me, I
expect to make up the time by taking work home tonight. If
you happened to look at the rest of my Day-Timer, disregard my housing association's Neutered Pet Task Force
meeting on Wednesday afternoon. I was never planning
to attend that. Well, I should get back to work . . . time
is money.
Your faithful employee,
Ken

P.S. I put the pencil holder in your in-box. Do you like it?
I figured blue was your favorite color.

1:30 P.M.:
Ken,
Thanks for the pencil cup holder—I'll put it next to the
God's eye you gave me last year. I noticed you put up a Girl
Scout Cookie sign-up sheet on the break room wall. Didn't

you get my memo last year about fund-raising in the build-ing? We outlawed it after you told the new-hires that buying your magazine subscriptions was part of their job descrip-tion.

Jerry

1:55 P.M.:

Dear Sir,

Does this mean I have to refund everyone's money? Your wife bought ten boxes. She said she was celebrating after losing ten pounds. Congratulations. Can I borrow the pencil holder this weekend? I need to show it to the kids as an example. I'll take good care of it.

Sincerely yours,

Ken

P.S. That was my best God's eye. Can I borrow that, too?

3:05 P.M.:

Ken,

When you were discussing diaper rash in the copier room with Delores, I put the pencil holder and the God's eye on your desk . . . next to the peewee soccer line-up you did on our letterhead. Did you need matching envelopes, or are the kids fine with our plain ones?

Jerry

3:19 P.M.:

Sir,

I can't imagine how my soccer stuff ended up on letterhead. I probably accidentally had a couple sheets at home when I

did this, and I wasn't paying attention. Can I have tomorrow afternoon off? I just received word that my son is being
awarded Best Handwasher at school. (No gifts, please.)
Your #1 employee,
Ken

P.S. You are welcome to mention the handwashing award in
the company newsletter—do you need a photo of my son
showing off his hands?

4 P.M.:
Ken,
Congratulations. I bet you and your wife are very proud.
Imagine, Best Handwasher two weeks in a row. Unfortunately, I can't let you off this week. I am certain your son
will understand since you were there last week to see him
lather and rinse for the entire student body. By the way,
thanks for the video of it.
Jerry

4:45 P.M.:
Jerry,
I'm not feeling very well. I wanted to give you a heads-up
that I probably won't be coming in tomorrow. I think I have
one of those nasty 24-hour things.
Ken

P.S. If I have to throw up on the way home from work, I
promise I won't vomit in your pencil holder (just in case you
were worried about that).

4:51 P.M.:

Ken,

Isn't it odd how illness can come on just like that? There
you were, well enough to attend your son's hygiene demon-
stration, and now this. I felt bad that you couldn't go to his
award ceremony due to work, and now you can't do either.
Don't worry, I'll send someone to take pictures at your son's
school. That way, you can rest easy and get better.

Your boss,

Jerry

4:59 P.M.:

Thanks Jerry. I'm feeling better. I'll see you tomorrow.

Ken

P.S. I accidentally stepped on your pencil holder, and the
God's eye broke when I used it to pry the can back into
shape. Sorry.

Being sick is actually a hot button with my employer. I have
been sick a number of times throughout the years because of
the various illnesses my children have brought home from
school and, therefore, I've also missed a lot of work.

At first, my boss was sympathetic, but starting this year, I
began detecting some frustration.

In February, I called him from home: "Sir, I don't want to
alarm you, but I may be going to that great coffee break in the
sky."

"What's wrong?" he asked.

"I'm sick."

"Again?!"

To me, "again" sounded a lot like: "Well, I certainly hope it's painful!"

I told my wife this, and she said it was probably the nausea talking.

"I don't have nausea," I replied.

She shook her head. "I meant his."

When I returned to work, I began to notice subtle messages.

"Where's my desk?" I asked.

"I gave it to the new-hire in accounting," my boss said. "I thought you were going to be out a long time. You can use that desk over there."

"That's an old typewriter table," I exclaimed.

"Doesn't it fit in your cubicle?"

"Where's my cubicle?"

Each day I missed work, the less friendly my boss became.

Finally though, in the spring, I hit a lucky streak, and I stayed healthy all summer long. In a fit of joy, my boss bought me a new desk. He even took me to lunch and praised me for my efforts at work. I told him I really appreciated his support in my time of darkness, and I promised him that it was clear sailing ahead.

Then, last week, there was a freak virus outbreak at my son's day care, and in the early morning light, I think I saw Jesus.

The strange thing is, when I called my boss to tell him to "give my desk calendar to someone needy," he didn't sound upset.

"I'm sorry to hear about that," he explained. "By the way, you are out of sick days."

I dropped the phone in shock. I had no choice but to drag my embattled, feverish body to the office.

There, I sat quietly all morning in my cubicle, gathering up enough energy to paperclip something together. After lunch, I did the same, only I got to stretch my legs occasionally when I walked to the bathroom to vomit.

It's not that my boss didn't care. Once, he tapped on the bathroom door to ask how I was doing.

"It's coming out my nose!" I shouted.

Oh well, what can I do? As long as my boss is happier that I am at work, that's what's important . . . the loud hacking noises notwithstanding.

Of course, the thing you need to know about my boss is that he doesn't have children. It's not easy working for some-one whose only real life experience is 80-hour workdays and racquetball on the weekends.

I have discovered that childless people tend to resent those of us with kids. I was surfing the Internet the other day and found a site called "No Kidding." It's a place for people who don't have children and "don't want to listen to those of us who do."

Can you believe that? There are actually organized groups around this country formed to offer support to those who feel victimized because they think that parents like us talk too much at work about our children.

After I calmed down, I decided to send an e-mail to the chapter president, to shed a little light on his problems. I wrote:

Dear Confused,
    I'm sorry, did I miss something? Has paradise broken out all over and now parents are treated to finishing complete sentences, eating unmolested food, and napping for more than five minutes before being the object of a dog-pile?
    I didn't think so.
    If we talk about our children, it's only so we don't go

crazy. Somehow, I don't imagine you needing to vent after a refreshing bubble bath or a lie-down before dinner.

I think you have the whole support system backward. Who cares if you have to hear a few words about diaper rash or SAT scores? What about us? It's absolutely devastating to listen about your week in the tropics sipping Mai Tais on a deserted beach.

Who needs the therapy here? Who gets the worst of it?

It only seems obvious that your announcement of a shiny, new, red sports car would do far more damage to us than what you might feel listening to any discussion about my son's stomach virus.

In conclusion, I hope you consider these points the next time you are at work, talking about your fun weekend dancing under the stars until 3 in the morning. The rest of us, who are in bed by 10 with teething babies and dishpan hands, have feelings, too, you know.

A couple days later he wrote back: "We rest our case."

I think these childless co-workers also don't realize the financial burdens on parents—especially the younger ones trying to make ends meet with $800 day care bills and a constant revolving door of infant formula and diapers.

For me, it seems a trade show always rolls around right after I have spent a fortune on seasonal clothes for the kids . . . and nothing is left over to revitalize my wardrobe.

I have often discovered that Dad is near the bottom of the food chain when it comes to receiving new clothes—just before Mom but right after the dog.

Therefore, while most of the single and hip people at a trade show look fabulous in their designer fashions and matching socks, I tend to represent the fashion underworld—you know: frayed pant cuffs, outdated trends, worn-out shoes.

To make matters worse, my co-workers are always dressed to the nines. Ron's pants are top-of-the-line. Bill wears bright, silk ties. And Jane has a new dress for every day of the show. I'm lucky to have socks without holes in them.

There are lots of booths at a convention. While some business actually gets done, most of the time, people just walk around checking out everyone else's setup (sort of like cruising the streets of Fort Lauderdale during spring break). All day long, other conventioneers dropped by our booth, read our name tags, and greeted the four of us with enthusiasm.

"Hi, Ron."

"Hi, Bill."

"Hi, Jane."

"Hi, What the Cat Dragged In."

I try to pretend they aren't talking to me, but that's hard to do while I'm trying to inconspicuously pull out the underwear up my back end.

Technically, we are all specialists in our field, and each person has a reason for being at the show to represent the company. We were hand-selected by our organization to work as a team. That's a good feeling, until at the last trade show a security guard wandered by and asked my co-workers if I was bothering them.

"Do you know this guy?"

Later, I took my turn walking around the convention floor. It is common for companies to hand out bags of promotional materials and samples to people at trade shows. I was handed trash.

After the first day, over a couple beers, I complained to my co-workers about my style.

"You look fine, Ken," Ron said.

"Yeah," Jane added. "I can barely see your chest hairs through your white shirt."

I went back to my hotel room feeling despondent. I called my wife. "Honey, I feel like I'm at the zoo, and I'm that baboon with the funny butt."

"It's just a phase," she said. "One day, we'll both be well-put-together and the envy of everyone."

I hope this happens soon, because next month there is another trade show. And I am bound and determined to get through that one without being yelled at by the sanitation crew for putting the trash in the wrong can.

The other thing I have discovered about myself when I am away at a trade show is that a business trip always sounds like fun—at first. It seems like a golden opportunity to escape from the mundane, ordinariness of my life as employee, husband, and father, and hole up in some plush hotel with the TV and bathroom all to myself.

But just like the last time when I was away, about halfway through the meetings, I begin to get that lonely feeling inside. That's when I jump on the phone.

"Hello?"

"Hi, Alasdair," I said cheerfully into the phone to my son. "How's school?"

"Fine."

"Anything exciting happening?"

"No."

"What are you doing?"

"Talking to you."

"No. Before that."

"Nothing."

"What are you doing tomorrow?"

"Nothing."

"Was it sunny there today?"

"I guess."

"Would you like me to hang up now?"

"If you want to."

I rolled my eyes. "Is your sister there? Why don't I talk to her now. You sound like you need a lie-down."

I heard the phone clatter on the counter.

"Hi Daddy," my daughter's enthusiastic voice came over the phone line.

"Hi Claire," I answered.

"Where are you?" she asked.

"In downtown Dall . . ."

"Deanna Cooper threw up at school today."

"Was she sick?"

"No, Devin Gilpin made her eat chalk dust."

"How do you make someone do that?" I asked.

"He hid it in her sandwich."

I stared at the phone. "Didn't she notice it and spit it out?"

"You can't spit out food in the cafeteria," she asserted.

"Why not?"

"Because they won't let you. Duh."

"So she got sick right there in front of you?"

"Uh-huh. Dad, I don't think I can ever write on the black-board again."

"I . . . is your mom there—maybe I should talk to her now," I said, feeling pale.

"Okay. I'll get her."

Only, she didn't. Instead, I heard her chasing the cat and then fighting with her brother. Next, I heard what sounded like two bicycles colliding into the dining room table.

Finally, my wife's voice came onto the line. Only, she wasn't speaking to me.

"Who left the phone off the hook?!" she shouted. "What am I now, your servant, too?!"

Click.

I sat there on the end of my hotel bed, staring at the dead phone.

I felt much better.

This phone experience, however, is nothing like what I get when I'm in my office back at work. There's something I have to get off my chest: Telephones should come with child safety locks just like prescription medicines.

The reason is quite evident—if the phone manufactures would concede, maybe I could actually get something done. Otherwise, I will continue to hear those dreaded words every day when I pick up the intercom on my phone: "Ken, your son is on line one."

During the summer months and in the afternoons after school, my kids call me—while I'm in a meeting—with important questions like:

"Dad, can the dog take a shower?"

Or, "Dad, what do I smell like?"

Or, better yet: "Daddy, I just ran into the door and swallowed my loose tooth. Mommy said the Tooth Fairy would probably pay up even before I pass it. Guess what 'pass it' means?"

Now, for those of you who have answered the "pass it" question while there are clients sitting in your office sipping a hot beverage and staring at you while you attempt a normal expression, you will understand when I announce that I have memorized the exact number of days until my children go to college.

You will also know the standard response passed down

through the generations of fathers to their children in situations like these: "Why are you calling me—where's your mother?"

I have discovered, however, that children call their fathers when they can't locate their mothers. And so, as the moms of this world step into their bathrooms, or are away from their desk at work, or hide under the house for some peace and quiet, dads are called away from their staff meetings to referee fights, grant permission for friends to spend the night, and tell baby dolls to "listen to your mother and take a nap right now!"

Once again I had the typical summer. The kind where my secretary wonders out loud who she works for—my kids or me. Certainly my boss wonders the same thing.

So, the other day, I laid down the law and told my children not to call me UNLESS there's no way they can ask their mom the same question.

The reprieve lasted exactly fifteen hours. Then my son called.

"Where's your mom?" I asked him.

"She's locked in the car."

"Don't you mean locked out of the car?"

"No," he explained. "She's in the car."

"Why?"

"I don't know—I was drying my shoes in the microwave and she just sort of flipped out."

"What?" I asked.

"Yeah, I know," he said incredulously. "I think Mom thinks we can't see her, but who else would be in the backseat under the dog's car blanket?"

I paused to catch my breath. "So where's your sister?"

"She's in the garage tapping on the car window. I have to relieve her in ten minutes. If Mom stays out there all day, can I eat the Jell-O right out of the box?"

And so the cycle continues until they go off to college—or, as I like to say, 3,654 days, 18 hours, and 46 minutes.

My family once had the bright idea that I should spend a day working from home. What better time, they thought, than summer, when I could "leisurely work" in the presence of my entire family.

When I mapped out that day, I had imagined working diligently in my den until I took a mid-morning cookie snack with the kids. After that, I'd return to my computer until my wife prepared a picnic in the backyard. Later, I would sit at my desk watching my kids play with the neighbors on our front lawn. Finally, I'd knock off an hour early and go for a family walk around the block. I even joked to myself that if I liked it so much, I just might telecommute for the rest of my life.

Yeah . . . right!

During the first hour of my workday, I barely touched a shred of work. The children kept running into my den to tell me important things like:

1. Knock-knock jokes.

2. Who touched whom first.

3. Why Mommy screamed really loud when she saw the mess in the playroom and is now lying down on the floor of her closet . . . with the door barricaded.

Sometime, around 10:30 A.M., I decided to take that mid-morning cookie break. Moments later, I walked into our bedroom, banged on the closet door, and asked my wife what happened to the Oreos.

"I told the kids to leave you some," she said opening the closet a hairline.

"There's one."

She sighed. "That's something."

"It would be," I said, "if the cream filling wasn't scraped out of it." I held the cookie to the crack. "Whose teethmarks do these look like."

She wasn't any help, so I returned to my den and began writing. That is, until my wife walked in.

"What's the matter?" I asked. "Got tired trying on shoes?"

She frowned. "Are you busy?"

I collapsed my shoulders and moaned.

"I need to run to the store," she continued.

"And?"

"And, I lost my keys somewhere in the closet—I need you to help me look."

I mumbled to myself all the way upstairs through the search for the keys and then back to my desk.

I think I managed to paperclip some papers together before my children inquired about lunch . . . thirty-eight times. After telling them over and over again to wait until their mom got home, I finally tacked a sign to my door that read: "Ask Someone Else!" That worked really well; up to the point that the neighbor called to ask me where my kids might find their mother and did I really have amnesia.

I told him to send them home. Frustrated, I slapped together peanut butter and jelly sandwiches for the kids and myself. We ate in front of the TV. Just as I was cleaning up, my wife walked in.

"Sorry, I'm late," she said.

"Where were you?" I huffed. "I haven't done a single thing today!"

"I was at the grocery store."

"For two hours?"

"I ran into Barb from Toddlercize," she explained. "She's really depressed—her baby has crib head . . . she needed to be held."

I headed for the door. "That's it, I have to go back to work," I announced.

"Why?"

"I left something there."

"What?"

"My sanity."

Of course, that day at home doesn't even come close in comparison to the majority of my days off.

Just once I'd like to take a day off without it exhausting me.

I'm not talking about partying till I drop or being tired from jet lag after vacationing on a tropical island. I mean worn out from climbing in the car and running errands to more places than Federal Express stops in a day.

Why do I look forward all month to a day off only to be A. woken at the crack of dawn and treated like a chauffeur (minus the tips), B. told my music "is embarrassing" and could I please put in the Back Street Boys CD one more nauseating time, and C. given a play-by-play of who's on who's side, who's touching who, and who's about to throw their shoe out the car window?

It's almost enough to make a second job look restful.

Take, for example, the last time I skipped a perfectly good workday, complete with final inspections, stressful deadlines, and arduous staff meetings, to accompany my wife and kids on a full set of errands.

We began our safari at the toy store so my daughter could pick out a present for her friend's birthday party. Every time she grabbed a toy and I said, "That looks nice," she'd shake her head no and put the toy back. We made five complete rotations through the store. Finally, I gave up and joined three other worn-out parents in a Monopoly game behind the blocks.

Next, my wife said she needed to run into the grocery store "for five short minutes to get a few things." The moment she left, the kids declared World War Three on each other with me positioned haplessly at the front lines.

My wife returned an hour later with a lunch bag, half full.

"You mean to tell me that while I sat here developing an acute spinal injury from the kids kicking the back of my seat, you've been inside the store buying that?!" I yelled, pointing to her small sack.

"No, I was talking with Rachel from PTA in the frozen food section," she explained. "Her son is lactose intolerant—she needed a friend."

I shook my head and tried to start the car, only to discover my battery was dead due to the fact I had a classical radio station blasting to drown out my children's fighting.

Finally back on the road, the kids were winded from their battles in the backseat and they wanted a snack to regain their strength. Their mother reminded them "We just had lunch an hour ago when we stopped to let Daddy have a nervous breakdown." They cried and screamed until I threw them two sticks of gum and a cherry cough drop melted to the wrapper.

Finally, I had to stop at the hardware store and I was bound and determined to go in alone. I wasn't inside more than two minutes enjoying the calm and tranquility before my wife was beeping Morse code on the horn: "Send reinforcements. The kids have mutinied." I rushed outside to find her lighting a flare and screaming "Medic!"

8

That's the Spirit!

"If all the year were playing holidays, to sport would be as tedious as to work."

—Shakespeare

"Okay, okay," I said, reeling from the pressure as my wife and I gathered around the dining room table, "pass the protractor and pencils."

She stood up and ran to the junk drawer.

"And get more erasers!" I shouted after her. "A lot more."

She returned with poster paper and tape.

"Put the chart on the wall," I suggested, grabbing the pointer from the floor. "Let's bar chart here," I said referring to the alphabetized list, "and then graph these coordinates before putting them on the spreadsheet."

"Honey," my wife interrupted.

"Hmmm."

"I think we miscalculated over there. Are you sure that is right?"

"I'm positive. I distinctly remember going to your parents' last Thanksgiving, so this year it's my parents' turn. Just refer to Table A: Easter 1999." I paused while she flipped through the binder looking for it. "Do you see how we spent both Easter and the 4th of July at your brother's house? That means we owe my sister a Christmas Eve and my folks a New Year's."

"So Christmas Day is at my parents' house this year?"

I nodded. "Yes, but we have to stop and see my folks from 1 to 2 P.M."

"But we'll be with them the night before at your sister's."

"This is true," I answered. "So do you want to call and say God told us in a dream last night that Jesus' birthday plans have been canceled, or should I call and break my mother's heart?"

She shook her head and began tabbing 1992's holiday notes for the archives. "Wasn't it easier when we just went to both parents' the same day?"

"And had two dinners?"

"Yeah."

"It did mean less planning, but the hospital bill for my stomach pumping was hard to swallow."

My wife booted up her computer files. "Okay, let's move on to what we are supposed to bring. For Easter we brought a salad. For Mother's Day we made a dessert. So this time, it's our turn to bring . . ."

"Say rolls—please say rolls."

"A vegetable tray."

"That's the most complicated thing to bring," I complained. "All that chopping."

"You have to have an appetizer."

"But people only eat the carrots . . . the rest goes to waste."

My wife shook her head. "I don't remember throwing out that many veggies last time."

"That's because your mom used the cauliflower to scrub out the turkey pan."

We finished highlighting our mileage and tacked it to the wall.

"What do the charts say about the dishes?" I asked. "Is it our turn to do them . . . because I swear it's your aunt Golda's turn."

"Auntie has a herniated disk, Ken."

"Yeah, well, she doesn't have any trouble hobbling back and forth to the buffet line with that shovel she calls a spoon . . ."

"Ken!"

"Well, why can't we just stay home this holiday season? Didn't our parents go through this when they were our age?"

"Yes and they complained about it every holiday as they loaded the kids and candied yams into the Pontiac and drove halfway across the state to take out the trash and hear about Uncle Fred's hardware business."

"Then why are we perpetuating the traditions?"

"Because," she said, "we'll be even worse and expect our kids to spend every holiday with us, including Flag Day, Passover, and Daylight Savings Time."

"I suppose we should pray they marry orphans, huh?"

The holidays seem to put perspective back in our lives as parents. Just as everything seems to be going wrong, a celebration pops up, making us feel good to be alive. Here's a look at some of my favorites:

New Year's:
New Year's Day has a funny way of halting us in our tracks to reflect on the past and hope for the future. It's also a time when my wife and I repeat our vaudevillelike routine. One of

us will inevitably say each December 31 that we should go to a big party and celebrate.

In this case, it's up to the other person to bring the reveler down to earth. This year it was my turn to be the party-pooper. Here's the picture I painted for my wife:

The evening begins with drinks, dinner, and dancing as our children are home with a TV dinner and baby-sitter who makes more an hour than I do. Then, I continued to tell my wife, as the clock strikes 12, confetti falls around us, we sip our third or fourth champagne, and we embrace for a happy kiss. Of course, the last thing you'll be expecting during that lovely moment will be standing in your living room at dawn the next day playing London Bridge Is Falling Down with two hyper children and a pounding headache.

What led up to the nursery rhyme game, however, is especially chilling.

Having arrived home around 2 A.M. that morning, you'll fall right to sleep, and the next thing you'll know, you'll be peering through hazy eyes at our son standing by the bed at 5 A.M. with a huge grin on his face.

"Hi Mommy," he'll exclaim. "Do you want to play a game?"

You will squeeze your eyes together tightly and nod.

Slobbering with excitement, he'll ask "What game are we going to play?"

"We are going to play the whisper game," you'll say in a raspy voice.

"YEAH! DAD, WE'RE PLAYING THE WHISPER GAME!" he'll scream, bouncing you out of your covers. "LET'S PLAY RIGHT NOW! HEY, MOMMY, WHY ARE YOU CLIMBING UNDER THE BED?! IS THIS HOW WE

PLAY THE WHISPER GAME?! LOOK DAD, MOMMY'S STUFFING DIRTY SOCKS INTO HER EARS!"

I, of course, will moan a little and then roll the other direction.

"MOMMY, WHERE ARE YOU GOING?" our son will continue to shout as you crawl out from under my side of the bed and burrow beneath my pillow.

"Allison, it's your turn to entertain the children," I will announce, not in any way sympathetically. This will shock you for many reasons, but mostly because it's the same person, whom, just hours before, showered you with New Year's affection. Then, I will lower the boom: "I took care of the kids last Saturday morning when I let them dog-pile on me in the living room while you slept."

Poking your lips out from under my pillow, you'll argue: "That doesn't count—we didn't stay out late last Friday night."

"That's true," I'll reply, "but the kids gave me rug burns on both knees. You're it."

Grudgingly, you will stand up, swearing under your breath. As you walk toward the bathroom, our daughter will leap into the bedroom, banging a pot with a wooden spoon shouting: "HAFFY NEW WEE-R!"

Caught off balance, you will most likely run into the doorjamb.

"Are you okay?" I will ask, not because I care, but because if you suffered a debilitating injury, it could force me out of bed.

"I'm not sure," you will reply from the floor. "Am I lying on my back or my face—I can't tell."

As you lie there on the floor in a stupor, it will suddenly oc-

cur to you that you've never seen this on one of those Champagne commercials. As your mind begins to clear, you'll hear your son exclaim: "DOG-PILE ON MOMMY!!"

Needless to say, my wife enjoyed a quiet New Year's Eve at home . . . again!

Of course, New Year's also comes with that dreaded need to improve ourselves . . . I just hate that! I don't know why I put such stock in New Year's resolutions, but I feel guilty if I don't at least try to have one. Like any red-blooded parent, the part of my life I feel the most challenged about is raising children.

So this year, I told my wife I wanted a New Year's resolution aimed at being a better dad.

"So what do you want to do better?" she asked.

"I was thinking about how I interact with the children."

"What does that mean?"

"Well, I raise my voice too many times."

"Does something else work?"

"You aren't helping."

She walked over to me. "Listen, why don't you ask the kids what they think before picking something that doesn't matter to them?"

I liked that idea. A little while later, I returned.

"What was their idea?" she asked.

"They want a later bedtime."

"That's a resolution?"

"Not a good one," I answered. "Our kids had no idea what a resolution was. So I took advantage of a teaching moment to explain the whole process and how it needs to be about me."

"What did they say?"

"They don't care when I go to bed."

She grinned.

I decided to go with not raising my voice. I even wrote it down on a notecard and pinned it on the wall next to my bed. Beginning January 1, I changed my ways. All in all, I thought the first two hours were relatively easy, mostly because I watched football.

Before long, however, I was confronted with misbehaving children. Without shouting, I had a difficult time getting their attention.

I tried stamping my feet, snapping my fingers, clearing my throat—nothing helped. Finally, I grabbed a Happy Meal whistle and blew really hard. It didn't get the kids' attention, but the cat has had better behavior since then.

By early afternoon, I was doing all I could to keep the words inside me. When I wanted to yell, I covered my mouth, bit my tongue, munched a handful of crackers—I even slapped myself. It hurt.

I also kept catching myself before I shouted. I'd go: "Ack," or "Wha," or "Yah."

The kids noticed this and said something.

"Dad, are you okay?" my son asked.

"Yes. Why?"

"It's just that you were making funny noises."

"So?"

"So, that's how the cat sounds just before she vomits a hairball."

By late afternoon, I was sweating under the strain. I tried really hard to keep my voice down when I caught my son bouncing on the furniture.

The house came to a standstill. Everyone was staring at me.

"What?" I asked.

"You just shouted," my wife replied.

"No I didn't," I said. "I was talking to myself."

"Do you often yell at yourself to stop horsing around?"

I nodded. "I'm a very bad boy."

Finally, nineteen hours into the New Year, I lost it completely when my children punched a hole in the playroom wall.

"Dad, I thought you weren't going to raise your voice anymore," my son said.

"That was before I knew you'd do something like this!"

"So, should we discuss bedtimes?" he asked.

I nodded. "Yeah. Bedtime is now!"

Oh well—wish me luck next year.

Of course, I'm sure my resolutions will always fail—just like my other one for this past year. I promised myself I would go to the gym and begin a weight-lifting program. It's actually a repeat resolution. I joined the YMCA last year but stopped going after the first day when some Herculean gym rat took a look at my muscles and asked if I was a recently freed POW.

I guess the trouble I have with my resolution is the intimidation factor. It's embarrassing to lift weights in a room where everyone is bulging with muscles and I look like a plucked chicken—free range.

"Well, what's your biggest fear?" my wife asked me when I told her about my resolution.

"That someone's great-grandma is going to outlift me," I told her.

"Is that really the end of the world?"

"It is if she does it with one hand and the other hand on her walker."

"Ken, everyone has to start somewhere," my wife explained. "You have nothing to be ashamed of about your body."

"Oh yeah? Have you seen my legs?"

"Is that what's bothering you?" she laughed. "Let me remind you that some guys look good with skinny legs."

"Yeah, ducks."

"Okay," she continued, "what's wrong with your arms then?"

"Besides atrophy?"

She gave me that "you're overreacting look." "Honey, why don't you look on the bright side," she exclaimed.

I squinted. "Bright side?"

"Sure. After a couple months, you'll start to pack on some muscle and . . ."

"They'll no longer call me 'The Stick'?"

Despite my intense trepidation, three days later, I actually went to the gym. I wasn't about to let another resolution bite the dust. When I returned home, my wife greeted me with enthusiasm.

"So, big muscle man, how did it go?"

"Well," I said, clearing my throat. "It got off to a rocky start."

She frowned. "What happened?"

"I was lifting two barbells over my head . . ."

"Yeah . . ."

"And my face was turning red . . ."

"Uh, huh . . ."

"And my eyeballs were bulging out . . ."

"Go on . . ."

"And that's when I dropped the weights on someone's water bottle."

"You did?"

I nodded. "It drenched some lady's socks."

She flinched. "What did you say?"

"I lied—I told everyone a fly flew into my mouth."

My wife smiled reassuringly. "Okay, that's not so bad—it was your first day. What else happened?"

I sneered. "They nicknamed me Hog."

"They did? Because you're so tough?"

"No, because I snorted and grunted a lot."

"When you were lifting the weights?"

"No, after I dropped the bench-press bar on my chest and I couldn't move."

"Oh."

"I'm going to go upstairs and pass out now," I announced.

"Alright. Dinner's at 6."

I think I'd be a whole lot happier if I didn't let resolutions get in my way.

Valentines:

I was licking my twenty-third Barbie Valentine envelope last February 12 when my daughter asked me: "How do you know Mom loves you?"

A more sentimental man would have smiled, pushed back a tear, and said, "Because she bore my children," or "Because she is my soul mate." I tend to measure love with a more practical ruler.

"There are many reasons I know she loves me," I told my daughter. "She loves me enough to grab a Barney sticker off my blind spot before I go out of the house.

"She loves me enough to make you kids call me Uncle Ken when you're acting like animals in public.

"She loves me enough to not laugh when I'm yelling hysterically at you to stop touching my food.

"She loves me enough to hand me a Pop Tart as I rush out the door and then call my boss to say I'll be late.

"She loves me enough to listen to my rants about the day care bill.

"I know she loves me because she checks my lapel for dried spit-up.

"She loves me enough to make me soup when you bring a killer virus home from school.

"She loves me enough to let me sleep through a midnight feeding.

"She loves me enough to make sure I have enough sunscreen on my bald spot.

"She loves me enough to have coffee standing by in the morning.

"She loves me enough to hide the last cookie for me to eat after you've gone to bed.

"She loves me enough to make all my worries go away with a cheesecake and a fork.

"She loves me enough to stay home on a Friday night and veg in front of the TV even though she'd prefer to go out dancing.

"She loves me enough to let me sleep in on days other than Father's Day.

"She loves me enough to take you kids for a long drive when I need a time-out.

"She loves me enough to let me write about all of this stuff in my column.

"She even loves me enough to say I look sexy in a mini-van."

I smiled. "Does this answer your question?"

My daughter shook her head. "When I'm married, I'm not going to do all that. I'm just going to give my husband a kiss."

"Yeah, that's good, too."

Of course, Valentine's Day always stresses me out. After thirteen years of marriage, I've bought my wife all the obvious gifts a husband can buy. I am simply out of new ideas.

So this year, I decided to ask an expert—someone who has received gifts for a long time: my mother.

I explained my dilemma to her. She ran me through the checklist.

"Have you bought her flowers?" she asked.

"Check," I answered.

"Jewelry?"

"Check."

"A stuffed animal?"

"Check."

"What about one of those naughty nighties? I always wished your father would have bought me one of those."

"Mom—stop!" I exclaimed. "A son wants to picture his mom in a long flannel nightgown—not on the cover of a Victoria's Secret catalog."

"Your father bought me underwear instead," she continued, frowning. "The tummy kind."

"I thought we were discussing me."

"Romantic getaway?"

"Check."

"What about chocolates?"

I grimaced. "She'd kill me. She's dieting."

"I love chocolates."

"Hence the reason you didn't get the naughty nightie."

"Sweet-smelling bath gels?"

"Check."

"Grapefruit spoons?"

I creased my eyebrows. "Who'd give grapefruit spoons for Valentine's Day?"

"Your father."

"Do you even eat grapefruit?" I asked.

"No," she replied. "I use them to clean the soles of my golf shoes."

"We don't seem to be getting anywhere here," I exclaimed. "Is this the best you can do?"

My mom thought quietly for a few moments. "Why don't

you buy her a coffee cup with hearts on it, or a Valentine mouse pad?"

"I hate those novelty gifts," I retorted. "They're embarrassing."

"Why do you say that?"

"Because, last year she bought me a pair of I Love You boxer shorts—silk. They sat in my drawer collecting dust until one fateful day when I was out of clean underwear."

"What's so bad about that?"

"By afternoon, I forgot I was wearing them."

"So?"

"So, before I knew it, they were the only thing between me and ten other guys in the locker room at the Y."

"What did you do?"

"Flexed, mostly. I also threw them away and went home without them."

"But lots of people like those things."

"I know," I agreed. "A couple weeks later, I saw some guy at the Y wearing my boxers."

"A new purse?"

"Check."

"Designer dress?"

"Check."

St. Patrick's:
In mid-March, I reminded my son that St. Patrick's Day was coming up, and he'd better not forget to wear green. "You don't want to get pinched to death by your friends," I warned.

He seemed nonplused by my advice. "If I forget to wear green, my teacher will paint a shamrock on my face to protect me."

I couldn't believe what he was telling me. When I was a kid, all a teacher did on St. Patrick's Day was send you to the nurse when your welts started to bleed.

"Not wearing green was like wearing a sign on your back that read 'Kick Me,'" I told him. "Even the gym coach would pinch us."

"Couldn't you sue for that?"

"No, but the kindergartners were allowed to cry."

My son also told me that students these days have to sneak around on the playground to pinch kids because school rules forbid such behavior.

"Not in my day," I retorted. "They sold tickets and printed a program guide. 'Step right up ladies and gentlemen—come see Little Kenny Swarner mutilated by his peers. If he doesn't wet his pants, you get your money back.'"

The teacher on playground duty had a front-row seat.

I can still vividly remember St. Patrick's Day 1974. I was in the third grade, and I forgot to wear green in an unforgiving school.

I recall how traumatic it was to stand by the coatrack trying to devise a way to see my tenth birthday. As I tried to look inconspicuous, I could sense the other kids searching around the classroom like a pack of hungry wolves for the green-less lambs.

I still have nightmares about it.

Of course, some kids back then would try anything to avoid a beating. The one thing no one with half a brain did was claim they were "unpinchable" because they were wearing green underwear. In the days of my youth, underwear came in one style for boys: white and tight. It would be a mistake of gargantuan proportions to say your underwear was green—a boy might as well say he was wearing a green bra. Getting pinched lasts one day. Green underwear heckling could still come up in a high school yearbook: Ken Swarner was voted "Most likely to wear embarrassing undergarments."

My only real option in the third grade was to hide. During recess, I stowed away in the coat closet. At lunch, I ate my sandwich in a toilet stall. Finally, as the end of school neared, I realized I'd need an exceptional escape route. With 15 minutes left in the day, I jammed a pen cap up my nose.

I remember feeling especially victorious sitting in the nurse's station with an ice pack on my face, waiting for my mom to pick me up. After all, it's not every kid who survives St. Patrick's Day without wearing green.

When my mom arrived, she lectured me for five minutes—a small price to pay. As we were leaving, the principal asked if I was okay.

I nodded, trying to mask a smile behind the cold pack.

"Uh oh," he announced, walking up to me.

He obviously noticed my swollen nose.

"You aren't wearing green," he continued. He pinched me so hard that the pen cap shot out of my nose like seeds from a tomato.

My son tells me it's cool to wear colored underwear these days. He's so lucky!

Easter:
One of the true joys of parenting, something that positively balances the kicks to the back of my car seat and unflushed toilets, is watching children frothing with excitement over the holidays. It's fun to see their eyes double in size in anticipation of Santa Claus coming down the chimney or the Easter Bunny hiding colorful eggs around the house.

So imagine my surprise when I walked into my son's room last Easter Eve and found him sketching out battle plans like Schwartzkopf before Desert Storm.

When I asked what he was doing, he started to cry. Apparently, my son not only hates the idea of a large bunny rabbit walking around in his house, but he thinks this bearer of holiday cheer is going to touch his stuff. Therefore, while other kids were dreaming of chocolate eggs and mountains of jellybeans last Easter, my son was staring wide-eyed behind his overturned mattress armed with a large stick.

I took the weapon away. "Son, this is supposed to be one of the happiest days of childhood."

He said it's been bothering him for years.

I tried to ease his mind. "The Easter Bunny has cute, floppy ears and a polka-dot bow tie," I explained. "He's not armed."

"Are you sure?" he asked.

"Well, I think we would have heard if he had a police record. We'd have seen his furry little face with the button nose on a most wanted poster at the post office."

My son was not satisfied.

"Well, can't you do something so he doesn't come in the house?"

"You mean have the egg hunt in the driveway?"

He shook his head. "Maybe he could leave everything on the front porch."

"So what are we going to tell your sister? The Easter Bunny isn't hiding eggs inside the house because your brother filed a restraining order? Is she supposed to go to sleep tonight thinking that if the bunny steps one paw inside, we'll stick his little cottontail in jail?"

He nodded.

"Okay . . . does that mean you are getting up at the crack

of dawn to bring the eggs inside from the porch, then hide them so your sister doesn't suspect anything?"

He nodded again.

"That sounds like fun," I exclaimed. "As your sister hunts for the eggs, you can pretend you don't know where to look. Mom and I will jump up and down, clapping every time you find one."

I thought he'd see the ridiculousness in the situation. Instead, he asked if he could call the police right now.

Finally, I had to tell him. I had to shatter his little childhood world and explain how the process really works.

"Son," I said, "you need to hear the truth. The Easter Bunny actually knocks at the front door and I let him in the house. While he hides the eggs, I stand watch to make sure he doesn't make any long-distance phone calls, eat our food, or play with your toys. I also frisk him before he leaves."

He stared at me.

"Do you feel better?" I asked.

He nodded. "Could you do the same to Santa?"

I assured him I would. What can I say? It's better than an Easter egg hunt in the garage.

Finally, I submit some Easter haikus written by a childless relative after a big family dinner.

Sitting on toilet
Kids searching for Easter eggs
Forgot to lock door

Nipple confusion
Irritable bowel syndrome
I hate parent talk

Round pink ham looks good
Sister breast-feeds at table
No longer hungry

Nephew with dimples
Jell-O splattered on my shirt
Damn that little brat

Unwrapped Easter treats
Chocolate stain on my butt
Doorman gives strange look

Halloween:

I must have asked my eight-year-old daughter a hundred times
if she was sure she wanted to go into the haunted house. Every
time, she nodded yes emphatically.

Feeling a little apprehensive, I took her into one last Halloween, and, as her fingernails dug into my wrist, I was absolutely amazed she wasn't pleading to leave. That is, until we
rounded the first corner, someone jumped from the shadows,
and I let out a blood-curdling scream.

What can I say? I was caught off guard.

The reason this haunted house adventure was not an intel-
ligent thing to do is, up to that point, my daughter assumed I
was the brave one. I would protect her. No matter how much
I tried to reassure her that everything was still fine, she stood
there looking at me as if zombies had just removed my brain
stem.

That's when my daughter's legs went wet-noodle and she
started to scream.

Suddenly, the strobe lights, moaning, laughing, and haunt-
ing sound effects completely overstimulated my senses. I felt

claustrophobic. I must have panicked, because the next thing I knew, I was trying to push back toward the entrance, shouting, "Coming through, coming through, little girl about to pee her pants." Only the crowd was so thick, there was no getting through the throngs of giddy people enjoying a good fright.

The more I tried swimming upstream, the more the wave pushed me back toward the ghouls and goblins.

To make matters worse, I was totally dismayed when the pathetic yells of a voice screaming for a "little compassion" turned out to be mine.

I gave up and started moving with the crowd, only my daughter didn't like that plan. Screaming at the top of her lungs, she threw her body to the ground. While recording this pitiful image, my brain also replayed my wife's parting words to me when I told her I might stop at the haunted house on the way home from ballet class.

"Ken," she said emphatically, "don't you dare take our daughter to a haunted house! It will scare her to death!"

(Isn't it funny how sometimes God makes dads look like fools? I wish he made moms do that, too.)

Anyway, I guess my daughter being on the floor began to create a bottleneck at the front door, because moments later, the house manager showed up to talk to me.

"What?!" I shouted at him. "I can't hear you! I think my daughter's screams shattered my eardrums! Hold that flashlight to your face and mouth the words slowly!"

He told me I needed to get my little girl off the floor and keep moving.

I explained to him that was impossible. "Don't you have an emergency team to help get kids out quickly in a situation like this?" I asked. "A quick-reaction force or something?"

"No."

"That's not very helpful," I complained.

"Well, maybe your daughter isn't ready for this and you should have stayed outside."

"That's good advice," I retorted. "Maybe you'd like to come over later and help my wife say 'I told you so.' You could stay for dinner."

Finally, I grabbed my daughter, told her to bury her face into my chest (she did the same with her teeth), and I ran really fast through the haunted house.

I'd tell you what my wife said when I got home . . . but I don't want to scare anyone.

Speaking of scary, kids don't really know exactly how frightening Halloween really is.

I'm not talking about the freaky masks, haunted houses, or pumpkin prices, but rather, the enormous amount of candy that exchanges hands during this season.

Have you noticed the first bag of Halloween candy is opened around October 20 and stays with us well through Thanksgiving? It's like Jesus' fishes and loaves.

You can't avoid it. There is one Halloween party after another. There's the school carnival, the shopping mall treats, the grocery store samples, and the drive-thru bank-teller handouts; followed up by the relatives' care packages and the kindergarten class hoedown; which are really appetizers for the neighbor's potluck and Grandma's house where the chocolate flows like the River Kwai; though nothing will ever compare to those final minutes as we waddle home to devour the leftovers from all those kids who never showed up at our door.

Especially sickening is that I'm right there, begging for handouts. That's why I told my wife, after the kids are in bed, I'm going to my Halloween party as something from Cinderella.

"The prince?" she asked.

"No, the pumpkin carriage."

To make matters worse, the life span of Halloween candy is practically eternal. After each event in October, the candy comes home and is transferred from small treat bags into larger containers on top of the refrigerator.

Then, throughout November, each night, the Dots, gum, and yellow dye #234 are dragged down to the dinner table where each child can pick two pieces for dessert and one for the next day's lunch. While my two children begin debates, trades, and consultations that rival any marathon work the United Nations might accomplish, my wife and I create diversions and complex plots so we can steal the premium candy bars when the kids aren't looking.

The candy summits last through Thanksgiving, when finally, Mom or I, depending on who has gained the most weight, announces the madness must end before someone goes into a diabetic coma. Because it is the last call, each child is allowed to pick five pieces of candy, which in turn means each parent can indiscriminately sneak twice that amount.

Now, one might expect the candy is either thrown away or included with the Goodwill pickup, but in all truth, it is hidden behind the ice cube trays in the freezer and is slowly consumed throughout the winter until my wife and I are whisked off in a moving van to the Betty Ford clinic.

I told you Halloween is scary!

Thanksgiving:

My love affair with Thanksgiving began as a child. Lying in bed on a crisp, cold November morning, I'd listen to the early sounds of my mother laying out the ingredients for the feast.

Next came the clinking sound of bowls, pans, and dishes

being carefully arranged on the counter in an orderly fashion as she staged her assembly line.

Then, as the early morning rambled along, the first smells would float down the hall—the aroma of piecrust or sautéed celery or fresh-baked bread. These wonderful fragrances would literally lift me out of bed. Getting dressed in warm, cozy clothing, I would pad down the stairs to the kitchen for a bowl of cereal and quiet conversation with my mom.

After that, I would grab a thick blanket and saddle up to the TV. You could always count on the networks to show *Charlie and the Chocolate Factory, Chitty Chitty Bang Bang,* or *The Wizard of Oz.* It was a tradition I loved. While those movies played, I'd steal into the kitchen intermittently to snitch a taste, trying to stay clear of my mom's deliberate pace as she moved about gracefully cooking, setting the table, talking on the phone to faraway relatives, and adding the final touches.

Soon, the doorbell would ring and the family and friends would pour in out of the cold and into every warm corner of the house. The football game was turned on and the appetizers began to flow like water. My mom would talk quickly, my dad took drink orders, and my brother and sister and I sat on grandparents' laps and answered silly questions. During the glorious meal, I'd sit back for a moment of reflection, soaking in all the excitement.

I remember it like it was yesterday.

This year my wife and I will prepare the Thanksgiving Day meal. We will wake up before it is light outside and realize the turkey hasn't defrosted completely. While it soaks in a warm bath, I'll run around frantically looking for the health department's number to ask about stuffing and e-coli because I had thought I heard something recently on the news. Then, I'll make my first of seven trips to the grocery store that day as we discover we are out of cinnamon, baking powder, milk, olives, eggs, ice, and a turkey baster.

As the 4 P.M. witching hour approaches, my little children will dissolve into uncontrollable tears. As my wife settles them down, I'll run a quick rag over the bathroom, moments before the first guests arrive. Hanging their coats on the spatula I'm holding, these dear friends and relatives will rush over to the TV and crank the volume up on the game next to my no-longer-sleeping nephew. My wife will make excuses for the mess, my mom will insist my dad cuts the turkey, and my kids will hop like kangaroos from one relative's lap to the next. Finally, during the meal, I will sit back for a moment of reflection, soaking in all the hubbub.

Best of all, my children will grow up loving every minute of it!

Except, maybe, for those children forced to perform Thanksgiving Day plays in front of their families. For those children, here's a form letter they can copy and present to their parents:

Dear Mom,

Even though I said I would never speak to you again and then slammed my bedroom door, the following letter is a formal complaint regarding last night's Thanksgiving Day play you forced me to participate in with my younger cousins.

What a travesty to put a thirteen-year-old boy through on what is supposed to be a day of thanks. Did you consider my feelings?

I was totally embarrassed wearing the pilgrim outfit—especially taking into account that Cousin Rachel was in the room watching. She's sixteen. Didn't you realize the kind of teasing a teenager is capable of doing? Maybe for Easter you'd like to finish me off by dressing me up as Little Bunny Foo-Foo.

I am curious about several things regarding the Thanksgiving torment:

1. Were you and your sisters sitting around over coffee one day thinking of ways to get us kids back for putting our elbows on the table, tracking mud into the house, and not saying thank you? What's wrong with time-out? Or a kidney punch? I am in the seventh grade—isn't it enough that I have peer pressure, homework, and chores to handle? Did we have to add six toe-head cousins playing pilgrims and Indians to the mix?

2. Who wrote the play, and whose idea was it that Capt. Standish (me) and Pricilla (Cousin Jane) would kiss? What kind of sick grown-ups think it's cute to make cousins smooch in front of everybody? I'm not taking chances with your mistletoe next month. I'm bringing Agent Orange.

3. Why did I ALSO have to play a Native American Indian and wear the loincloth? I don't care what you say (and my friends would testify to this), it's underwear. The little bear paw prints on the butt only made it worse.

4. Do you think Aunt Luella will really scream "Way to go Massasoya" at my high school graduation like she said she would? I'd have a hard time explaining that to my friends . . . that is, until Uncle Eddie rolls the video

of me pretending to plant corn in the loincloth underwear.

5. You also told me that my older cousin John would be in the play. Isn't it convenient that he threw up after dinner and watched the play from the couch with a cold washcloth over his forehead and a smirk on his face? Did anyone think to search his pockets for the wishbone he OBVIOUSLY used to tickle his gag reflex? Unfortunately, all I could think to say to get out of the play was that I had diarrhea. It didn't occur to me that Grandma had a twisted sense of humor and a bottle of Pepto Bismol.

6. What's next on your holiday agenda? Is this year's family Christmas card a picture of me in Barney jammies? Maybe you could find a photo of my first bath—which would look nice with a snowflake border.

My lawyers will be in touch.
Sincerely yours,
(Insert name)

Finally, I wish there was such a letter those of us who eat too much could send as a means of apology to our Thanksgiving Day hosts.

The last time I overate, all I could see beyond the faces peering down at me were a couple patches of ceiling and several shadows created by the flickering of light from the holiday candles. Moments before I had been enjoying a Thanksgiving feast, and now, I was stretched out on the floor, so stuffed I couldn't even move.

"Ken, can you hear me?" my wife shouted into my red face. "Blink once if you are okay, twice if you are not okay, or three times if you think you might vomit before I can pull my face away."

"He blinked four times," my dad exclaimed. "What do you think that means?"

"Maybe he wants to see a priest."

"Well then someone wipe the cranberry off his face —let the poor man die with dignity."

"How did this happen?" I heard someone ask. "Did anyone see it coming?"

There was a lot of chattering. I wanted to tell them it wasn't anyone's fault—my eyes were just bigger than my stomach. I couldn't concentrate on the words—I felt dizzy and confused.

"The last thing I remember him saying to me," my sister interjected, "was: 'Are you going to eat the rest of that roll?'"

My wife looked around the room. "Let's put him on the couch."

"Not on my good couch," my mother protested. "Put him in the bathroom, or on the deck, or even upstairs on the guest bed with everyone's coats—you can claim your husband when it's time to go."

"What if we put a blanket down on the couch?"

"Or a tarp."

I wanted them to leave me on the ground, but I didn't know how many times to blink for that request. Before I knew it, I was hoisted onto the couch.

"Those mashed potatoes are probably expanding in his stomach," my dad announced. "The gravy makes them do that."

I was about to motion for a pen and paper to write I would be fine, when someone suggested taking me to the hospital to have my stomach pumped. As I blinked madly, my uncle Albert offered to jump up and down on my stomach for half the price.

"I can probably pop him like a zit," Albert explained. "It's going to be gross—the weak shouldn't watch."

With that repugnant comment, the moms in the room recognized a ripe opportunity to lecture their offspring. "Do you see what can happen when you eat too much?" they shouted. "You end up like your uncle Ken here—nearly comatose with mashed potatoes swelling in your stomach and your uncle Albert ready to pinch your guts out."

Suddenly, my stomach made a loud gurgling noise. Everyone froze as if the slightest noise might detonate my body. I think a couple of them prayed.

Even my brother showed some concern: "I'd advise everyone to stand back—that belt of his looks like imitation leather—it could shatter. Get the kids out of here. No reason to discolor their Thanksgivings for the rest of their lives because they can't shake the image of Uncle Ken blowing up."

My eyes doubled in size.

"Maybe we should call an ambulance."

My mother's face lit up. "Does anyone know how much he ate?"

"Why?" my dad asked. "In case the paramedics ask?"

"No," she answered. "I want to write it down in Ken's baby book."

"Under first gluttony?"

Finally, miraculously, I lifted my head and belched.

Then it was time for dessert.

9

No Expense Spared

"Life is a progress from want to want."
—Samuel Johnson

I don't know what happened between the time I was a kid and when I became a parent, but something certainly changed. As far as I am concerned, whoever is responsible for deciding that kids should get everything they want should have hell to pay.

Take for example, birthday parties.

When I was a kid, the moms in my neighborhood had the same birthday game plan: eight friends, pin the tail on the donkey, and a lopsided Duncan Hines cake. No one worried about spills, because the décor of those days matched the Kool-Aid colors.

Simple is no longer in fashion.

These days, it's not a child's birthday party without a clown that spits fire, or treat bags holding seventeen pounds of candy. As each birthday passes, the bar gets raised. I recently went to one of our friend's parties where they hired a singing princess for their daughter. It just so happened that Cinderella also read the grown-ups' palms while the birthday girl opened her gifts.

When my daughter's birthday party was on the horizon, I decided to put my foot down and tell my wife we weren't going overboard. The only way I could have topped the palm reader was to hire a masseuse who also created balloon animals. I wasn't about to spend that kind of money.

"We aren't competing with the other families," I explained.

"I agree," she exclaimed. "Some of those parties are getting ridiculous."

"So ours will be small and inexpensive?"

"I didn't say that."

"What does that mean?!"

"Ken," she replied. "In the last year, your daughter has been invited to a princess party, teddy bear tea, sleepover at the zoo, and a pool bash."

"So?" I retorted. "That doesn't mean we have to go crazy. Why don't we have an old-fashioned party in the backyard—you know, like the ones we had when we were kids?"

"What—hot dogs and a Slip 'n' Slide?"

I nodded. "One of my favorite memories is running and diving on a Slip 'n' Slide."

"I'm sure it is," she said coldly. "So what should I write on the invitations—'Come to our party and get grass clippings all over yourself,' or 'Warning, this party may cause grass burns'?"

I frowned. "Well, just promise me we aren't doing what the Franklins down the street did," I demanded.

"You mean for their daughter's birthday?"

I nodded.

"I thought the luau with hula dancers and roasted pig was a blast."

"Maybe," I said, "but Al had to dig a hole in his backyard to cook the pig and then he had to put all that dirt and grass back afterward."

"That's not so bad," she argued.

"Oh yeah!" I countered. "Now, every time Al mows his lawn, it smells like bacon."

"So?"

"So, their dog is constantly drooling all over their expensive lawn furniture."

My wife looked nonplussed.

I paused for a moment as the reality of the situation began to sink in and I saw the truth for the very first time. "When it comes right down to it, I really have no say in this, do I?"

She smiled. "Not if your next idea is hamburgers and lawn darts."

My dad had it so easy!

If that wasn't enough, how about the times I've spent party-favor shopping? The first time my wife and I glanced through a party catalog with our son. As I was turning a page, my son's eyes grew huge as he pointed at the page of firefighter decorations. "Look at these firefighters! I want to have a fire engine party!"

I examined the cake decorations he was pointing at. "What do we need those for?" I asked. "They're $2.95 each."

"They go on the cake," my wife explained.

"Do you get a discount from the baker if you supply your own decorations?"

"No."

"Well then forget it."

"But I want toys on my cake," my son cried.

I scoffed. "What about all of those Happy Meal toys you have under my bed? Isn't there a theme under there we could use?"

"I want firefighters!" my little boy demanded.

Then, my wife got that gleam in her eye—the look that makes my wallet start to shiver.

"You know," she said, "I saw a great cake idea the other day for firefighter parties."

"Don't say a real Dalmatian," I exclaimed.

"No, better than that."

I shook my head vehemently. "Fire trucks cost millions of dollars."

She ignored me. "It's a cake that looks like a seven-story building—it catches on fire."

"Real flames?" I asked.

"Uh, huh. You spray a fine mist of brandy on the outside of the cake," she explained. "It actually burns for a couple seconds—sort of like cherries jubilee."

"Brilliant—we can get the kids drunk. How are you going to explain that when you run for PTA president?"

"The alcohol burns off, Ken."

"Brandy costs 30 bucks a bottle," I pointed out. "Isn't that a little elaborate for a preschool party?"

"You don't think a room full of four-year-olds would be impressed with a flaming cake?"

"Impressed?" I echoed. "How about so scared they pee their pants."

"You think so?"

"Sure. Instead of treat bags, we could hand out Pull-Ups."

"I think it would be one of those parties you'd talk about for years."

"Yeah, in therapy," I replied. "Then, when our son has his own kids and asks me about his fourth birthday, I can say, 'the reason you don't remember it honey, is because I took you to a hypnotist to block out the nightmares. Haven't you always wondered why your daddy doesn't have eyelashes? They burned completely off. I'm sorry, where was your mom during all of this? Stomping out the cat.'"

My wife and son stood there looking at me as if I needed a sedative.

I realized I was fighting a losing battle. "Firefighters it is," I exclaimed, surprising them. "After all, who am I to bring up a couple of pesky insurance concerns?"

Needless to say, we did the Towering Inferno for my son's birthday, and it was a huge hit with the kids and their parents. To top that, my wife is talking about landing a helicopter in the backyard for my son's next birthday.

That will be fun. I've been meaning to get that extra part-time job anyway.

The second time I helped plan a party was when my daughter was turning three and my wife wanted me to help her find decorations.

I agreed to do it, feeling excited that my child was old enough to have parties with kids her own age.

That Saturday we set out early for the Paper Kingdom: The Ultimate Store for Party Animals. "So, what's our budget?" I asked nonchalantly as I parked the car.

"I'd rather not focus on a number," my wife answered. "Let's concentrate on what we need to buy."

"Easy," I replied. "Eight plates, napkins, forks, cups, a packet of invitations, and some party hats."

"Plus wall decorations, streamers, balloons, cake decorations, treat bags, name tags, prizes, games, candy, and a yard sign," she added.

"All that?!" I complained.

"Ken, parties cost money."

"Fine. But how are we going to afford all this?" I argued.

My wife shrugged. "We might have to cut back on our grocery money this week."

"What, like hamburgers instead of steaks?"

"No, like brisk walks instead of dinners."

I felt feverish as we walked into the store. "I'll go find the party hats," I announced. A few minutes later, I carried the hats over to my wife. "Here, I found these."

She studied my selection. "Did you grab the cheapest hats you could find?"

"No. These are hi-tech party hats," I explained. "Look, they're triple stapled."

"They're foam."

"That's okay," I declared.

"And they're dark brown."

"I thought our daughter's theme was Old MacDonald's Farm."

"It is. So what are the girls putting on their heads: mounds of cow dung?"

"No," I argued, flipping the hat upside down. "They're tornadoes. I just have to figure a way to invert the hat."

"Well won't that be a happy thought for her birthday?!" my wife exclaimed. "Instead of a magician, I wonder if Rent-an-Actor could send a banker to foreclose on our daughter's farm just before cake and ice cream."

I put the hats back and kept looking.

After a while, my wife came over with a loaded shopping cart.

I blanched. "Is that all for our daughter's birthday, or did some of the neighbors ask you to pick up a few things for them, too?"

"Ken, our daughter only turns three once, you know. These

are the moments you don't get back—I'm not going to go cheap for her birthday."

I rummaged through the cart.

"What are you looking for now?"

"Where's the pin the tail on the donkey?"

"They don't do that game at parties anymore." She laughed.

"They don't?"

"No, they do things like scavenger hunts."

"Good," I exclaimed. "Maybe we can have the children canvass the neighborhood for groceries so we can eat next week."

She rolled her eyes. "What are you doing?"

"I'm writing out a scavenger list. How do you spell bologna?"

My wife left me standing there in the noisemaker section. Funny, but after that day, she never invited me to go party shopping again.

While birthday parties may seem like the worst, please consider the neighborhood get-together.

When I was a kid, a grown-up party meant all the kids in the neighborhood piled into the playroom with a can of pop (which we had to split), a small bowl of potato chips, and, if our folks were really generous, popcorn with extra butter.

Today at a neighborhood party, I count my blessings if none of my children fall into a diabetic coma before the end of the evening.

I still remember the first time I witnessed this smorgasbord.

A group of us decided it would be fun to get together and play cards. Among us, we had thirteen kids, all under the age of twelve. John and Betty Redenbacher offered their home, and we all brought snacks.

On the drive over, my son complained: "We're bringing pretzels? Couldn't we have brought Doritos or M&Ms or pop?" he whined. "Kids hate pretzels."

"No they don't," I argued. "Pretzels were a big deal when I was a kid. See, they have salt on them—isn't that neat?"

"No."

When I carried our snack into the Redenbacher's family room, the other children looked suspiciously at me.

"Look kids, pretzels!" I exclaimed, holding the bag up over my head.

"Oh good!" little Jimmy Redenbacher exclaimed. "Pretzels!"

"See," I said, turning to my son and smiling. "I told you."

Jimmy nodded. "My dog loves those. Here Blackie, look what Mr. Swarner brought for you."

Blackie nuzzled his nose into my crotch. "Don't mention it, Blackie," I said, as he snorted. As I scanned the room, my eyes went as wide as lollipops. On every imaginable surface top, couch cushion, floor space, and in every grubby little hand in that room, was every chip, dip, candy, pop, and treat found on the planet.

I called my wife into the room.

"What?" she asked, pulling herself away from the grown-up conversations in the living room.

"There," I said, pointing at the children. "Is it just me, or could we all be arrested for trafficking preservatives?"

"Where's our pretzels?" she asked.

"Over there," I answered. "In the dog's dish."

She frowned. "Before they start eating, maybe we should talk to our kids."

"About what?" I asked. "How it feels to have your stomach pumped?"

Before we could say anything, Betty Redenbacher walked into the room. "Don't be shy, dig in, and eat whatever you want," she told my son and daughter.

My wife and I exchanged glances. What could we do? We certainly didn't want to embarrass ourselves and make a scene.

So, I said, "Sure, live it up kids." After Betty walked away, I immediately grabbed the oldest kid in the room: "Here's a buck—watch my kids. If they start to slur their words, come find me."

When it was finally time to go home, we all walked into the Redenbacher's family room to claim our junkies.

"Is that our daughter over there?" I asked my wife.

"Where?"

"With her head in the Fig Newton bag?"

"No," she answered. "Ours is under the coffee table with Gummy Bears stuck in her hair."

I shook my head: "Okay, you take Courtney Love here, and I'll go look for Keith Richards."

Later that evening at home, my son turned to me and said: "Thanks, Dad, for letting us eat whatever we wanted tonight. We had a blast."

"You bet," I replied. "So, do you need to vomit again, or can I wash out the bucket now?"

I wonder what Child Protective Services would have to say about that?

Of course, none of this has stopped my wife from sending me Christmas shopping—on the early shift.

I swear, it was right after the energy crisis in 1979 that toy executives figured out that if people will stand in line for gas, maybe they'll do the same for toys. You know what? They were right. All it took was a couple companies to design a limited number of trendy items, and boom, every Christmas is now a nightmare for parents across the world.

Instead of toasty moments in front of the fire with a frothy glass of egg nog and carols on the stereo, moms and dads are driving across state lines to find the last Nintendo game on earth.

I can assure you, my parents would never have done that. My dad would have looked at my mom and said, "I'm not going to seven different malls, scour the catalogs, or fly to Cleveland to find a toy! Hell, I could probably make something similar to that in the garage with my circular saw."

"But it's a really cool toy!" I would argue.

"What's wrong with a simple toy for Christmas?" he'd reply. "Jeez, when I was a kid, all I had was a stick to play with—it was half a broom handle—it was my best friend."

This past December, I woke up at 5:30 A.M. and drove to Wal-Mart, because three days earlier, I stopped at the store and was told by the electronics manager that a limited number of the new, yet impossible to find, Pokémon Nintendo games would arrive Saturday morning.

I knew my chances of getting one would be determined by my place in line. The store opened at 9 A.M.

"Shouldn't you go earlier than 5:30?" my wife asked. "Maybe you should leave right after dinner on Friday."

I told her that was ridiculous—5:30 was fine. Besides, I didn't want to repeat what happened last year when I went too early, fell asleep, and someone, trying to steal my place in line, rolled me under a Dumpster.

Miraculously, this time I was the first in line, so I sat down with my back against the glass entrance door. Moments later, appearing through the morning's dense fog that hung over the parking lot like frozen whipped cream, was a mom bundled up in a ski outfit.

She stood facing me.

"Hi," I said.

"Hi."

It was obvious she felt a little uncomfortable standing in front of a darkened store with a man she didn't know. So I tried to break the ice. "Are you here for a Pokémon Game Boy?"

Her face brightened. "Yes, how did you know?"

"Well, I know Wal-Mart has white cotton briefs on sale today, but I went with my first guess," I exclaimed.

Next thing I knew, we are chatting up a storm as if we were old friends. As more and more people began to arrive and line up behind us, the camaraderie was better than anything I could have expected from midnight caroling downtown. People were showing pictures of their kids, discussing the holidays, sharing a breath mint—it was fun.

I'm not sure, though, what other people thought as they passed by us. Once, a guy with ACL-CIO bumper stickers on his car drove by, honked his horn, and yelled "Solidarity brothers!"

Because I was first in line, people assumed I was the veteran toy scrounger in the crowd, so a lot of questions were fired my way. They wanted to know about online shopping, the next hot toy, and my fallback positions.

One lady even asked, "So, what happens if we have to go to the bathroom?"

"There isn't anywhere to go," I explained. "You have to be prepared for that. You don't want to step out of line and lose your place."

"How did you plan on not having to go to the bathroom?" she asked me.

"Easy," I replied. "I haven't had any liquids for three days. When I'm done here, I'll go to the hospital and check into the dehydration unit."

Around 7 A.M., my wife called me on the cellular. "Is it cold?" she asked.

I chuckled. "Let's just say that each time someone new pulls up, we take turns running out to his car to de-ice our fingers on the warm hood."

"Well, what have you been doing?"

"Talking, mostly."

"That's it?" she said.

"That, and as the sun rose over the distant hills, we sang 'Kum Bye Yah.'"

Finally, at 8:55 A.M., the manager appeared with the keys to open the store.

We stood up as one mass, and I could sense the 200 people behind me in line. The store manager's eyes went wide as he peered out at the swarm of parents. Looking at my nose pressed against the glass of the door, I think he almost reconsidered opening the store, but I am pretty sure I inspired him to proceed when I said, "Hurry, I can't breathe!"

As the glass doors slid open, we moved like a giant tsunami toward electronics. I will say, everyone held their place in line, proceeding in an orderly fashion—except for an older lady who showed up just as the doors opened and tried to outrun the line. We all joined hands, forming a human chain, and forced her into a cosmetic display.

Reaching the sales counter, the electronics manager, who had told me days ago about the morning shipment, appeared panicked. I walked up to him, and in a triumphant voice said, "I'll take one Pokémon game."

He began to stutter. "They didn't come in, sir. But, we have lots of Loony Toones games. Those are really popular, too."

I looked at him for a couple moments as if he was something I couldn't identify on the bottom of my shoe. "What's your name?" I finally asked him.

"Todd."

"Todd, I want you to imagine something for me."

"Okay."

"Todd, picture a nine-year-old boy on Christmas morning. Can you see him? Do you notice that he's crying his eyes out, while, over by the discarded Loony Toones game, his dad is sticking large pins into a GI Joe with the name Todd taped to its head?"

Todd gulped. "I'm pretty sure our store downtown received a large shipment this morning," he said rapidly as if trying to plead for his life. "If you hurry, you'll get one."

Suddenly, my premier, number one spot in line meant crap. To make matters worse, at least the first ten people behind me overheard my conversation with Todd, and as I looked back, they were pealing out of the line. They were smart parents, however—not letting on to the masses what had happened so they could increase their early lead to the downtown store. As they jumped out of line, they made excuses like, "Oh my God, I think I left the stove on at home," or "Here, you take my place in line—it's the season of giving, you know," or "I got some bad fruitcake, I think I'm going to throw up."

I, too, began sprinting toward my car. As I passed the others in line, a few people shouted out "How many are left?" I didn't want to outright lie, so I pretended I didn't speak English.

I violated seventeen traffic laws on my way downtown. By the time I arrived, the line outside the downtown Wal-Mart stretched for three city blocks. I took my place behind a mom holding a sign that read "The end is near." I overheard one stressed-out holiday shopper passing by say to her friend, "Well Carol, it could be worse—we could be those pathetic people."

The line didn't move for three hours, so finally, I gave up and left dejected. For a solid week there wasn't a word from the underground regarding the next Pokémon score. Then, the following Saturday, I was watching a TV program on liver transplants. The doctor being interviewed said you can donate half your liver, and what is left, will actually regenerate itself in your body.

I hope so. I gave mine to an Argentinean man in exchange for a Pokémon game.

Funny, but this all-out effort to give our children the world even bridges over to toy shopping after the original onslaught of gifts.

Once, my wife and I dutifully followed our son (armed with birthday money) around the local Toys "Я" Us store.

After an hour, I paused to reflect with my wife.

"Why can't he choose something?!"

"It's a big store," she answered.

"All he does is saunter up and down these aisles picking up toys and putting them back again," I said. "Why does he do that?!"

"Maybe he's getting back at us for giving him underwear for his birthday."

"It wouldn't be so bad if I could wait at the front of the

store while he decides," I explained. "But every couple minutes he's calling me over to look at the features of a toy he has no intention of buying."

"He wants to be sure."

"And I think my foot fell asleep," I added.

"Well, maybe you shouldn't sit at the Barbie Tea Party table."

"I'm exhausted!"

She pointed. "He's on the move again."

I stood up and leaned into the plush toys. "I can't go on."

"He's on his way to the games," she announced.

"Please, leave me here to die with dignity."

"Dad!" my son called out on the other side of the aisle. "Come look at this!"

"What?" I shouted back. "Did you find someone's dad lying in the middle of the floor?"

"No, I found what I wanted. It's a Pokémon game."

My son appeared around the corner and started heading for the cashier. I reminded myself that the worst thing I could do at that moment was get prematurely excited just because it looked like we might be home before Easter.

As we neared the cash registers, I caught a glimpse of another parent also walking victoriously toward the check-out stand—her little girl's hands clutched around several packaged items. The mom looked like a death row inmate granted parole. Suddenly though, her daughter lost focus, dropped the toys, and wandered off toward the bed-wetting dolls.

Our eyes locked for a moment and I gave this mom a solidarity smile—a "we are all in this together" look.

I could have sworn she mouthed back to me the words: "Please, if you really care, take this giant Hello Kitty pencil I am holding and stab me between the eyes."

I was about to help her to the tea set when my wife called.

"We're moving again!"

"I . . . I thought he wanted the game," I stammered.

"No, he says he definitely wants the *Star Wars* toys."

I drew in a heavy breath and marched after them.

"Oh no," my son cried when he reached the action figures. "They don't have the Jedi Fighter. That's what I really wanted to buy."

"Are you sure?" I asked. "Is this your final choice?"

He nodded.

"SOMEONE GET MY SON THE JEDI FIGHTER!" I shouted hysterically. "JEDI FIGHTER IN AISLE FOUR!"

"Oh, here it is," my son said pulling it down from the shelf.

"Thank God," I moaned. "For a minute there, I thought we'd never get out of this toy store."

"Well, if we were trapped here," my wife said, "at least there are kiddie beds, various snacks, and Winnie the Pooh postcards so we can get word to the outside."

"Yeah, but it's not going to end like that for us!" I said happily. "We're getting the Jedi Fighter!"

"No we're not."

"What?!"

"Your son just put the *Star Wars* stuff back—he's off to electronics," she said. "I have dibs on the Ferrari bed."

I shook my head. "I'll go see if I can find some animal crackers for dinner."

After all this effort of buying, wrapping, haggling, and scrounging, what am I going to do? I'll tell you. From here on out, I have a new toy-buying policy. Gone are the days of fun and games for my kids. From now on, I'm only buying them gifts a thirtysomething newspaper columnist would get for himself.

This might sound cruel, but please understand. In my children's rooms, you'll find 12 battery-operated gizmos made in the United States of Disney; 7 dolls that do flips, repeat slang, or bleed for no apparent reason; enough railroad tracks to carry a windup train across the country; and 2,953 Happy Meal toys. Still, with all that stuff, my kids would rather play with my things.

I have fond recollections as a child enjoying my bright orange Hot Wheel tracks, reading *Hardy Boys* books, and listening to *Brady Bunch* records. I have shared these special feelings with my children to spark an appreciation for their own toys, only to be rebuked with blank expressions and rolling eyes. I suppose the cycle will repeat itself and their kids won't care how their parents whittled away hours of enjoyment with my toenail clippers, personalized stationery, and shoe polish kit.

I complained to my wife about this, but she didn't have time to listen. She was too busy interrogating the kids about her missing address book, curling iron, and salad tongs.

Once, my son asked me for a Vigilante Victor action figure.

"What? Are you bored with my tub and tile caulk?"

"I saw it on TV, Dad, and it's a really cool toy. I've got to have it!"

"I want my pillow back."

"Deal!"

Three days later I inadvertently mowed over poor Victor abandoned in the tall grass as I caught a glimpse of my son running to the neighbors wearing my "I Love You" boxers.

I made the final decision to stop buying my kids toys one month during a power outage. Suddenly, in the middle of storytime, the lights went out. For those of you with children under the age of eight, you'll appreciate what I mean when I say their loud, piercing screams disturbed livestock two counties away.

"Get the flashlight," my wife shouted, "before a window shatters!"

I stumbled to the junk drawer and fished for the light. The batteries were dead. I felt along the wall until I reached the garage to retrieve another flashlight: dead. I made my way to the glove compartment of my car. That flashlight was extinct, too. Even the tiny light on my key chain was deceased.

Back inside, my kids were running around in small circles crying in the dark as if Dracula would descend any minute. My wife had quietly left the room in search of a lobotomy.

"Ahhhh! It got Mommy, it got Mommy!"

"Do you see what happens when you play with my stuff?!" I shouted, waving the dead flashlights. "Now the vampire has taken your mom!"

"Ahhh!"

I told them I had experience in such matters and if they stopped playing with my things, I'd bring their mom back from the living dead.

"We promise, we promise," they sobbed.

Two days later I found First Communion Barbie discarded in the trash and my ski poles missing.

I haven't bought a toy since.

I am a little concerned, however, what I'll say when Christmas rolls around. Just how do you explain to kids why Santa brought them a briefcase, a spare tire, and batteries for the flashlights?

10

Family Togetherness

"There was an old woman who lived in a shoe,
She had so many children she didn't know what to do;
She gave them some broth without any bread,
She whipped them all soundly and put them in bed."

—Anonymous

There is nothing like some family togetherness on a weekend hike.

Of course, there is nothing like pinching your finger in a bike chain, either.

It's just that I can never understand why I get so eager about a hike. All week long, I'll talk excitedly about the big day. Even at the trailhead, I'm happily running over the last-minute details. But then, sometime around the first bend, right before one of my kids loses a sock in the river or jabs a walking stick into my ankle, I suddenly find myself on the Baatan Death March.

"I'm tired," my daughter said at Lake Gitchee Gummee.

"You can't be," I argued.

"Why not?"

"We haven't left the parking lot yet."

For the entire hike, "I'm tired" was my children's battle cry—except, of course, when they were running energetically into the woods past the signs marked "Stay on the Trail."

For the first mile, I had to keep telling my son to stop picking up foreign objects on the ground.

"I'm searching for treasure," he explained.

I knew it was only a matter of time before he inadvertently picked up the wrong thing. But, when he did, I tried not to alarm him. I saw no reason to make matters worse.

That didn't stop his sister from saying something. "Eeew, I hope you know, Alasdair, that you're holding deer poop!"

Sure enough, in panic, my son accidentally threw the doo-doo at my face—just like I knew he would.

I looked at my wife. "Any idea if deer poop will come off in the creek?"

Next, my daughter said she needed to go to the bathroom; however, she refused to go behind a tree.

"Would you like to be air-evaced to a gas station?" I asked.

"I wish I had to go," my son announced. "I've always wanted to know what it's like to potty outside."

"It's just like at home in your bathroom," I answered. "Only there isn't a toilet seat to hit."

Back on the move, my daughter stepped up and grabbed my hand. I noticed that other hikers passing by smiled as if a father and his little girl holding hands were the cutest thing they had ever seen. Little did they know she was actually just conserving energy by riding me like a rope tow—which wouldn't have been so bad if she hadn't also stopped abruptly every three minutes to pull a rock out of her shoe or pick a stick off the ground.

"Honey," I exclaimed. "Every time you stop, it pulls on my arm."

"So?"

"So, I think you dislocated my shoulder."

Finally, I called a halt to the march.

"Alright, who has my water bottle?" I asked.

"Here, you can use mine," my son answered.

"Thanks," I said taking a swig.

"Uh, Ken," my wife interrupted. "I think that had backwash in it."

"I don't backwash," my son protested.

"Yes you do—it has floaties in it," she retorted, grabbing the bottle from my hands and holding it up to the light.

"I know that," he replied. "It's moss."

"What?!" I yelled, looking incredulously at my family. "I've had deer dukie flung at me, and now I drank moss. Would someone like to finish me off with a large rock?"

"I will," my daughter exclaimed. "What's 'finish me off?'"

"Hey, look over there at that," my wife interrupted. "Isn't that a pretty bird?"

"Where?"

"Over by your dad."

"Where's Dad?"

"There," she said, pointing. "Headed back toward the parking lot."

Not to be left out of a trend, the Swarners instituted family game night on Fridays just like Parker Brothers asked the people of our nation to do. And you know, they were right. A good game of Monopoly does bring a family closer together.

In fact, after several weeks of landing on Boardwalk, going

directly to jail without collecting $200, and foreclosing on St. James, I've seen exactly how my family works. And because of this, I've managed to categorize those sitting around our little old board game.

There is . . .

The one who stares off into space unknowing it's her turn to roll . . . again.

"Whose turn is it?" my daughter asked.

"Yours," I replied. "That's why we've all been looking at you for the past two minutes. Sorry that was too subtle, would it help you next time if the rest of us chant your name as we build a human pyramid on the game board?"

The spouse who takes the game very seriously.

"Mommy, could you please pass the onion dip?"

"Quiet! I'm concentrating!" she snapped.

I blanched. "Allison, you're starting to scare me," I said. "That's the third time I've seen you consult the rules, and why do you keep checking to make sure I counted off the right spaces? I've never seen you this intense over a game before."

"Well, Candy Land isn't all that challenging," she explained. "Unless you count losing a turn on Gooey Gumdrops."

The cheater who denies any wrong-doing.

"I didn't cheat," my son wailed

"Yes you did," I pointed out. "You re-rolled the dice when you thought no one was looking."

"No I didn't—they fell out of my hand the first time—I wasn't ready."

"Really?" I scoffed. "I thought that since you prayed to God, spit on the dice, did a dance on the sofa—with your shoes on I might add—repeated 'Give me a six' 27 times, then let them roll completely across the board, you were ready to roll the dice."

"I forgot to have the dog lick them."

The whiner who wishes that just once you'd LET her win.

"Why do you always get to win?" my daughter complained.

"Well," I explained, "after spending $800 on your flute for band, freezing every weekend on the soccer sidelines, and doing your homework even though I already passed the fourth grade, all I have left is beating two children at Monopoly. It's sad, but I own Boardwalk and you don't. Now fork over $4,500."

The roller who applies too much spin on it.

"Where'd they go?" my son asked.

"Are you referring to the dice?" I replied. "Are you saying it wasn't your intention to skip them off the table and out the doggie door?"

"They went out the door?"

"Yes—didn't you hear the dog scream?"

The parents who don't know when to quit.

"Should we finish the game even though the children quit because they were bored?" my wife asked.

"Of course we are going to keep on playing," I answered. "While I buy Park Place, go order a pizza. Grab some chips out of the cupboard—we might be here all night."

"What about the kids?" my wife asked. "We told them an hour ago we would come upstairs and kiss them goodnight."

"They probably fell asleep," I retorted. "Do you want to trade Marvin Gardens for two railroads?"

I wonder if this is what the Parker Brothers intended?

The major benefit of having a family, of course, is that it's a built-in source of entertainment.

Our tent, however, is a different matter.

"We need a two-room tent," my wife said, standing in our

driveway, inspecting my packing job as we prepared to drive to the national park for our annual Memorial Day weekend campout.

"What's wrong with our two-man dome tent?" I asked. "We don't need to spend money to buy a new one—our old one is big enough."

"Our daughter's doll tent has more room than ours."

"Yeah," I retorted. "But when Barbie has a couple kids and she and Malibu Ken are struggling to make payments on their spiffy convertible and swank town house with the pink elevator, I don't expect to see them upgrading to a larger tent, either."

"Haven't you noticed that the kids have grown since last year?" she asked.

"Big deal," I pointed out. "We'll be so tired at night from hiking and swimming that we won't even notice the tight fit."

Once the tent was set up at the campsite, it was a little cramped—not that I was going to say anything. The four of us covered every square inch of the air mattress, which, in turn, covered the entire floor of the tent. Unfortunately, it rained right after dinner and we were forced to spend a little more time inside than I had planned.

"Well, see, this is nice," I said positioning our flashlight in the little change pouch hanging on the inside of the tent. "It's not every day a family can spend quality time all bundled up in a cozy tent. Anyone for a game of Uno?"

"Dad, every time you talk, it moves the mattress and spills my pop," my daughter complained.

"Give it to me—I'll hold it," I said. "Alright, now is everyone else happy?"

"No—the pop is running into my sock," my wife announced, grabbing my pillow to mop it up.

"Did you get it all?"

"I'm not sure."

"Well, is everything else fine?" I asked.

My son shook his head. "My pop just spilled, too."

"Hand it to me," I said, getting frustrated.

"Ow—Dad, your elbow hit my eye!"

"Maybe we should just go to sleep," my wife suggested.

That was easier said than done. It took us ten minutes to change our clothes without any bloodshed. We stretched and turned in the cramped space as if we were playing Twister. It was especially a challenge to change after our flashlight suddenly ran out of batteries.

"Honey, your foot is in my pajama bottoms," my wife said.

"It couldn't be," I explained, "my feet are over here in a puddle of pop."

"Then what's this lump in my pant leg?"

"It's me, Mommy!" my daughter screamed. "Help! I can't breathe!"

Finally, when everyone was dressed, we stretched out like four sausages on a hotcake. We said our goodnights and closed our eyes.

After a few minutes of silence, I exclaimed: "I can't sleep."

"Because there's a suitcase on your legs?" my wife asked.

"No."

"Because you're precariously poised on the edge of the mattress?"

"No. Because I'm still holding the kids' pop."

"Put the cans outside the tent," she instructed.

"I can't," I explained.

"Why?"

"Because if I move off this mattress, it's likely to flip over and smother the rest of you to death."

"That's it," my wife announced. "Everyone up—it's time to leave."

We drove the 200 miles home in silence.

Without the tent.

How my wife felt about that tent sums up how we both feel about camping after several seasons in the woods.

I know millions of Americans headed once again this past summer for their state and national parks to camp with their loved ones. Nestled campsite to campsite, these families hiked the interesting nature trials, ate their dinners on the open fire, and sang camp songs into the late evening.

The Swarner family was out there, too. My wife and I were the ones weeping in the Port-O-Potties.

My kids love camping, so I wouldn't deny them that experience, but between you and me, I no longer find camping a vacation.

Frankly, I don't get it. I go to the campsites just like everyone else. I have the high-tech camping gear. I have the citronella candles. I participate in the ranger-led programs. And yet, while all the other families in the park are getting excited as their Jiffy Pops near the point of explosion, my wife and I are running around like overworked Molly Maids trying to get everything done.

On the surface, I suppose camping sounds like a refreshing change of pace from domestic life at home. It's a chance to unwind and relax. But by the time I have removed all the rocks from the site, set up the tent, hooked up the propane, cooked the dinner, chased the kids out of the tent (again), sprayed on the mosquito repellent, and cordoned off a safe area around the campfire, I'm left wondering why I didn't just stay home and clean out the gutters.

My wife says camping is worse than poking out an eye with a marshmallow stick. Of course, the way my kids erratically jerk their sticks out of the fire toward my face with a flaming marshmallow on the end, I'm not so sure.

This Labor Day, however, I decided to camp with a new attitude to give it one last try. I'd go with the flow. If the tent got dirty, big deal. If we ate cold cereal for dinner, I didn't care. I planned to be Mr. Mellow and enjoy the vacation like everyone else—I even had my wife buying into the concept. I figured that as long as my kids wanted to camp, I should enjoy it.

So when the tent flaps were left open repeatedly the first day, I didn't freak out and rush around constantly closing them. I shrugged it off. Of course, the next morning, the park ranger said I had the most mosquito bites he'd seen in 30 years on the job. He even took my picture for the camp newsletter. I hope to see it when the swelling goes down.

I took a big gulp.

On the second evening, when my daughter dropped the four melted marshmallows she haphazardly squeezed onto one stick, I casually dismissed it—praising myself for remaining calm and cool. Little did I know, however, that she'd leave them on the ground so I could step in the goo later. By bedtime, I had seventeen leaves, a slug, two bird's feathers, and half of an old dirty diaper stuck to my shoe.

Still, I persevered.

The next day, when we were sequestered in our tent as it poured outside and the roof looked like it might cave in, I told my wife "Don't worry, this is part of the charm." I'd like to NOW take this opportunity to publicly thank those who returned our personal items that washed across the campground when our tent burst.

So, as usual, I celebrated the end of the camping season. And for those who camp next to my wife and I next summer . . . please excuse our tears.

Speaking of crying, I sure am tired of my lot in life as the family seat saver. I am the first to be ready for an event and I hate to be late, so I tend to be the one assigned to make sure everyone else gets a good seat at weddings, school plays, and Easter Sunday at church. Or in other words, I'm punished for being punctual.

It's so embarrassing to be the front-line person in this battle.

I sit there governing over a block of seats like an usher waiting for the king and his royal court to arrive. Meanwhile, every indignant mom and ticked-off grandma passes by my fortress and mumbles something under her breath about seat hogs or rude fathers.

That's why I finally told my mother I wasn't saving seats anymore. "If you want to see your granddaughter's hygiene play, you and the rest of the family need to arrive early."

"But you always save us seats," she complained.

"Not anymore."

"Did you know I gave you life without an epidural?" she retorted. "Can't you at least do this for me, just this one time?"

"I don't have a big enough coat to save a whole row."

"I was in labor for sixteen hours," she continued. "You gave me hemorrhoids the size of Volkswagens. Isn't that worth a little consideration?"

Feeling guilty, I cracked. "Alright, but this is the last time. Sooner or later, I'm going to get thrashed by an angry mob of room mothers."

I told my wife she needed to help me save seats.

"I can't," she shouted. "I'll be backstage for the play. It's my job to tell the dirty fingernails when to make their entrance."

I arrived at the school 45 minutes early and grabbed half of the front row.

I sat at the aisle to block off the entrance to the seats, and I put my shoe on the last chair I needed to save. That worked pretty well, until the janitor grabbed my wing tip to see if it fit him. So I took my sports coat off and dropped it at the other end. Then, I placed other items, like my belt, tie, and vest, down the row so people would know the seats were reserved.

Unfortunately, I didn't have something to cover every seat, so other parents walking into the auditorium would stop, and in a loud voice, shout, "Is that seat taken—the one over there between the Kleenex and the white cotton briefs?"

I should have done what another dad did. He laid Tic Tacs on every seat and then swatted little kids away with his playbill.

The thing is, people look cross when you tell them an entire row is taken, especially when it's just you sitting there half-naked. I always feel compelled to provide an excuse, other than, "I'm sorry, the rest of my family are deadbeats." So I lie and tell people that my mom is handicapped.

"She needs five to six strong family members to get her here," I explained. Then, I call my mom at home and tell her that she needs to limp when she walks into the auditorium, "preferably with loud moaning sounds."

At the hygiene play, she forgot. It's only a matter of time before hostile parents rub me out.

That is, if my own family doesn't do me in beforehand. I am, of course, talking about potlucks.

I was watching with great interest the preparations around

the potluck table during our annual summer get-together in my aunt Theresa's backyard when my wife and daughter walked over to me from the badminton net.

"Hungry, Ken?" my wife asked.

"A little," I said. "Why?"

"Because you are watching the food like a kid with his face plastered to a candy store window."

I blinked.

"Are you positioning yourself so you can be first in line?" she asked.

"No, I'm trying to match up the different dishes with their owners."

"Why?"

"So I know who to sue if I get hepatitis."

My wife looked perplexed. "What are you talking about?"

"I hate potlucks," I answered, keeping my eyes peeled forward. "I mean, why do people insist on getting together without the health department's seal of approval?"

"What's a health department?" my daughter asked.

"Let's face it," I continued, "a lot can happen in a kitchen when no one's minding the chef. We have no idea who might have sneezed into their casserole dish or tested the batter with their fingers. I think we should be cautious."

My wife rolled her eyes. "Okay, but how do any of our family know we didn't do the same thing?"

"We brought a bag of chips and store-bought onion dip," I answered. "I plan to have witnesses when I break the seal."

"It's a summer picnic, Ken. This is what people do. They go to barbecues and have potlucks."

"Great," I exclaimed. "I'll be sure to add that when I'm describing my weekend to the guys back at the office. I can hear myself now: 'It was great. I played a little volleyball, saw old friends, got the runs from Aunt Karen's bowl of ambrosia. You know, it's the first weekend I've dropped five pounds.'"

My wife felt my forehead. "Ken, it's awful hot outside—maybe you should sit in the shade for a while."

"I feel fine," I argued. I turned to my daughter. "I want you to stay away from Cousin Fred's three-bean salad."

"Why?"

"It's a judgment call."

"What do you suggest we do, Ken?" my wife interrupted. "Ask who prepared their food with rubber gloves?"

"That's not a bad idea," I exclaimed. "I was thinking we'd get in line after those who went first are done eating so we could find out who felt gassy."

"You'd really ask someone that?" my wife replied, the lines on her forehead bunched close together.

"No," I said incredulously. "I plan to drop little packets of Gas-X on the ground when no one's looking and see who desperately picks them up."

"I think I'll take my chances," my wife replied.

"That's fine," I retorted. "I'm sure an evening in Theresa's bathroom while we make S'mores over the fire pit will be memorable. Should I stand outside the window and describe the festivities to you, or would you rather sit quietly in there roasting a marshmallow over a scented candle?"

She didn't answer. Next year, I think I'll eat before going.

I suppose family togetherness is best defined during the holidays.

Every November, I can't help but fondly remember the year my wife and I hosted the Thanksgiving dinner in our first apartment (some might argue it was really a large walk-in closet).

Everyone from both sides of our family came, mostly, I suppose, to see if the fire marshal would stop by after dinner to arrest us for unlawful merriment in a restricted space (that, or they thought there might be a Guinness World Record in it and they wanted their names listed in the book).

My wife and I were still newlyweds when we volunteered our apartment, and we were excited to have our turn at hosting a holiday party. We talked about it for weeks—the menu, decorations, invitations, mood music, and the table setup. We figured it would be a little tight, but we assumed a few extra card tables would make everything work.

It's obvious that we had no idea that Thanksgiving in a one-bedroom apartment on a tight budget with limited cooking skills was worse than anything the pilgrims endured on their tiny *Mayflower*. At least, not until after the family arrived, and I happened to pass my wife in the hallway.

"We are running out of wine," she announced. "You need to run to the store and buy more."

"With what?" I asked. "We've already spent our grocery budget for the next three weeks."

"That's okay—we'll have leftovers to eat."

"That's what you said about the appetizers," I replied. "They're licked clean!"

"They are?"

"Yeah," I replied. "Have you noticed anyone stashing food in her purse? Maybe during dessert I should quietly excuse myself and check everyone's coat pockets."

My wife gave me that "look."

"Alright, I'll go," I said.

When I got back, I found my wife standing in the parking lot. "How's it going in there?"

"The kitchen is jam-packed with people," she replied.

"Are you okay?" I asked, noticing her flushed face. "Is everything alright?"

"Well, you know that little red button that comes with the turkey?"

"Yeah."

"I took the turkey out of the oven a little early, and just as I was barely squeezing past everyone, the button popped out."

"So?"

"So, it knocked your grandpa to the floor."

I stared in disbelief. "Is it time to eat?"

"I think so," she answered.

I announced dinner when we walked inside, and people started grabbing any open space they could find. Half the family sat at the makeshift table I had constructed with a series of card tables. As for the rest of them, my sister and her kids chose to eat on the couch, a couple of our nephews fought over the coffee table, my uncle Larry found room under the TV stand, and my wife opened the oven and managed to get three place settings around the oven door.

As I walked into the kitchen to grab the turkey, my wife pulled me aside. "Ken, the mashed potatoes aren't ready," she said with tears in her eyes. "I mistimed them."

I panicked for a moment, then regained my composure. "Well, serve them for dessert."

"Dessert?"

"Yeah, drizzle a little chocolate syrup on top and call them cream puffs," I explained. "I'll jack the thermostat up so everyone is too lethargic to notice."

All in all, by the grace of God, we not only fed everyone, but people seemed to enjoy themselves.

After the last person left, my wife and I surveyed the damage.

"I'm thinking that next year we won't do Thanksgiving at our apartment," my wife announced. "What do you think?"

"I'm not even doing Daylight Savings Time in this apartment!" I exclaimed. "Now, let's go next door and see if we can beg the neighbors for leftovers."

Speaking of Thanksgiving, I love my mom, but the woman can't roast a turkey. I'm really not sure what she does to it, but it's drier than sand. It's like our turkey has been frolicking in the harsh Arizona desert without sunscreen all summer long before the folks at Butterball caught up with him.

Last Thanksgiving, at halftime, when my mom was out of earshot, my siblings and I congregated around the cheese ball to discuss the impending meal.

"I think Mom has picked a turkey with a defective red button ten years in a row," I announced.

"I know," my brother added. "Doesn't she realize it's dry?"

"No," my sister told him, staring at me, "because every year, someone tells her how great the turkey was."

I blushed. "We can't hurt her feelings," I said, admitting I was the culprit.

"True, but can't we focus on something else?"

"Like what?"

"How about the cranberries?"

"They're from a can," I explained. "Maybe you'd like me to tell her how great the stick of butter was. 'Boy, Mom, the butter really made the meal. Was that the expensive kind?'" I looked at my sister. "I'm sure that would make up for the entire table hacking out petrified turkey meat into their napkins."

"Well," my brother interjected, "maybe one of us should volunteer to help out in the kitchen?"

"I tried that," I explained. "I called Mom yesterday and asked her if she needed me to come over and baste for her."

"What did she say?"

"She asked me why I would want to do that," I answered. "I told her that putting on a Thanksgiving dinner is a lot of work. So she told me if I wanted to be helpful, I could rake her front lawn."

"You did a nice job."

We were all quiet for a few moments and then my sister's face brightened.

"Maybe we should establish a patrol," she announced. "You know, take turns opening the oven and basting the turkey."

"What's Mom going to say?" I asked.

"She won't know," she answered. "We'll grab a couple cans of chicken soup from the pantry, a couple turkey basters, and whenever Mom leaves the room, we'll take turns opening the oven really fast and squirting the bird."

It was a great plan, and everyone was feeling much better, until it was my brother's turn and he forgot Mom had double ovens. He squirted chicken noodle soup on the sweet potatoes. We gave up after that and fought over who got to have the dog under their chair at dinner.

Of course, later that night, as I was putting my kids to bed, I felt bad for missing the point of Thanksgiving. I am thankful to have my mom, regardless of her inability to roast a turkey. After all, Thanksgiving is about appreciation and tradition.

So I reconfirmed these values with my children and explained how lucky we were to have a great-grandma. As I was leaving my son's room, however, I noticed he was chewing gum, and I told him to spit it out.

"It's not gum," he argued. "It's Grandma's turkey. The more I chew it, the bigger the wad gets!"

I wonder if Miles Standish had this problem?

Finally, a discussion of family togetherness wouldn't be complete without my favorite family memory: decorating the house for the holidays.

October 1 begins the holiday season at the Swarners—three months of decorating our rooms starting with cotton cobwebs, progressing to cardboard turkeys, and finishing off with plastic holly.

At the start of each month, we gather as a family around a big box of decorations and, one by one, take out each memory and lovingly place them around our home.

As we pulled the first plastic spider from the box last October, we once again renewed our yearly tradition.

"Mom! Claire won't let me hang up the Happy Halloween banner!" my son screamed.

Followed by: "Ow! Dad! Alasdair hit me with the rubber bat and I'm bleeding on my shoe!"

Diverting the fight, I suggest: "Why don't you kids each take one of these candy dishes and put them on the coffee tables downstairs?"

"I get the Frankenstein one."

"No! I want that one!"

"You can have the pumpkin."

"That's not fair—the color is all faded—it looks rotted!"

Next, my wife, who loves the holidays and gets really excited about decorating, returns to the box of decorations after stringing orange lights down the banister. "Who put the Dracula candles on the TV?"

"I did," I answered. "Why?"

"I moved them."

"After you told me to put the candles anywhere?"

"Well, I didn't think you'd put them there."

Meanwhile, the children had each other by the hair and their other hands locked tightly on the Frankenstein candy dish.

"Give it!"

"No!"

"Where do you want me to put this?" my wife asked, ignoring them.

I looked up to see she was holding the paper ghost on a string I gave her when we were first married. It is more gray than white and missing an eye. "The garbage."

"How about right there?" she said, pointing to the highest point in the house.

"You want me to put a nail in the vaulted ceiling so we can have a shredded ghost hanging on it for only four weeks out of the year?"

She nodded. "We'll put the paper pilgrim with the missing foot there next month and then the mistletoe for Christmas."

"It's too high up, " I replied. "Who'll know it's mistletoe? People will think we are forcing them to kiss under the Christmas mold."

Just as she was about to reply, the Frankenstein candy dish, which was held taut between my children's hands, went airborne and splintered into a hundred pieces at the foot of the stairs—candy corn flying into corners we probably won't vacuum until spring.

"You were right, dear," I said. "This is more fun than watching the football game."

She couldn't speak.

Needless to say, I sent my wife to bed, farmed the kids out to the neighbors for the rest of the afternoon, and then decorated the house with the remaining Halloween crafts, which my wife rearranged the following day.

11

Minding Your P's and Q's

"Children are natural mimics: They act like their parents in spite of every attempt to teach them good manners."

—Unknown

Modern medicine has given us test-tube babies, cancer cures, laser surgery, and new and improved aspirin coatings, but still, with all this technical wonder, can you believe the voice boxes on children can't be wired with volume controls?

I know, I asked my pediatrician.

My children came into this world with two sound levels: loud and asleep.

Knowing this, I have no idea WHY I thought it would be a good idea to take them into the office with me one day. I suppose right before I decided to do this, they were asleep in their beds looking all cute and everything.

The moment we stepped in the office door, though, my kids acted as if I worked in a Boeing wind tunnel.

"Dad, is this your desk?" my son yelled.

"Dad, do you get recess?" my daughter screamed.

"Dad, she's touching me!"

"Knock it off!" I hissed as I pulled them into the bathroom and closed the door.

"You are embarrassing ME," I said sternly. "People are trying to work HERE."

"It's not my fault," my son yelled, his voice reverberated painfully against the small, enclosed space.

"Is, too!" my daughter barked.

"Is NOT!"

"Dad, what are you looking at?!"

I glanced away from the mirror. "I'm checking to see if my eardrums are bleeding."

I lectured them for another three minutes. Finally, my kids agreed to keep their voices down if I'd take the wads of toilet paper out of their mouths.

As we opened the bathroom door, my son bellowed, "Man, it stinks in there!"

I was ready to shepherd them into the car when Marge in Accounting urged me to introduce my kids around the office. Grabbing my son's and daughter's hands, she ushered them from cubicle to cubicle.

"You have such well-behaved children, Ken," she remarked.

That's not saying much. When Marge brought her kids to work last month, they tipped over the watercooler.

Finally, I stopped outside my boss's door and looked at my son and daughter.

"If you guys embarrass me in here," I said through gritted teeth, "I'll sell you to that lonely, childless couple down the street whose dog just died! Understand?!"

They nodded.

As we walked in his room, my kids huddled behind my back giggling and playing under my sports coat. *At least they aren't yelling,* I thought to myself as they playfully tugged on my belt and pulled out my shirttail. I stood there trying to adjust myself and smile at the same time. Then, my daughter peeked her face around, and as my boss asked her about her favorite TV show, my son grabbed the back of my pants and shouted out my underwear size.

Excusing myself, I whipped them both into the car.

As we drove away, I jumped on my cell phone to call my wife.

"He announced my underwear size!" I told her. "My boss just looked at us as if we were mutants."

"Ow, Dad, you're talking too loud!" my son shouted from the backseat. "Can't you keep it down?!"

I suppose if volume controls are out, I shouldn't even ask the doctor about smart mouths.

Kids are loud, obnoxious, liars, tattletales, lazy, gross . . . it's amazing they've been allowed to stay on the planet this long. Unfortunately, it's our responsibility to turn these messy rug rats into something we can trust to go over to other people's homes and represent our good names.

I suppose that's why I called the obedience school.

"Hello, I'd like you to teach my kids better manners."

"Excuse me? Sir, this is a *dog* obedience school," the woman told me on the phone.

"I know," I said. "Just consider my son and daughter one of the litter."

"Are they slow?"

"No, grade-schoolers. It's just that they use their laps for plates, their hands for spoons, and their sleeves for napkins. How long will it take for you to train them?"

"I don't think they'd like our school," she explained.

"Are there snacks?"

"We serve milkbones after sitting exercises."

"They'd probably eat those—and the sitting program couldn't hurt. Do you use a rolled-up newspaper when they put their feet on the table?"

"Huh?"

"Isn't there something you can do?"

"I'm not sure I'm qualified to help you, sir," she continued.

"Do dogs lick food off the floor?"

"Yes."

"You're qualified. I've noticed dogs also chew with their mouths open," I said. "How do you deal with that?"

"We don't."

"Yeah, my wife is ready to give up, too," I explained. "She's on the edge—our kids carry food all over the house. She spent three hours last night vacuuming."

"Crumbs off the floor?"

"No, tacos in our bed."

"Tacos?"

"Yeah, the jalapeños made my eyes water all night."

"Have you tried talking to your children?" she asked. "Reason with them?"

"I told them I was getting my own apartment if they don't improve their manners."

"And?"

"My wife bought matching bath towels for our new place last night."

"Sir, you can't leave your kids home alone," she answered.

"People leave dogs by themselves."

"In kennels."

"Okay."

"Sir, that is appalling," she huffed.

"And my kids spreading mayonnaise with their fingers isn't?" Click.

Geesh. I was going to pay extra. So does anyone know the number to a good military school?

Or better yet, do you know how to cure a tattletale?

My son was dying to tell on his sister recently, but seeing that I didn't smell smoke or see S.W.A.T. teams fast-roping down my porch; I tried to ignore him.

Of course, this didn't satisfy the little Benedict Arnold, so he started to sing.

"I know a secret . . . I know a secret."

There is a good reason why I didn't want to know the secret. If I knew, I'd have to do something about it. And I learned a long time ago that it's better for the mom to know—she has to do something about it.

At this point, however, my son was frothing at the mouth and talking to himself like a mental patient: "I hope Claire doesn't flood the house—but, of course, it's not my problem," he said out loud. "Not like anyone cares what I think."

Flooding the house did sound like a problem, but again, I reminded myself, my wife was better with a mop. So before he could elaborate, I pretended that I had something in my eye and rushed off to the bathroom mirror.

My son followed me.

I locked the door.

He stuck his mouth under the crack and asked, "Does anyone else hear water running?"

I stepped on his lips.

He slipped a note under the door.

I acted as if I didn't see it—which was hard to do considering it was written on a grocery bag.

When I walked out of the bathroom, he looked sullen.

"I've got to tell someone," he whined.

"Tell the cat," I replied

"The cat doesn't care."

"Neither do I."

"Okay," he moaned. "I guess you don't care that Claire is flushing her Barbie down the toilet."

At that point, not caring instantly became a moot issue, because I not only now knew what was going on, but my wife will know I knew, too. So of course I had to get involved. I also had to put on hip waders.

Later, as I finished mopping the floor, my son walked in. "Why didn't you tell your mom about this first?" I asked incredulously.

"She doesn't like me to tattle."

"I don't like it, either," I complained.

"Well, you never told me that before," he replied. "I guess next time I won't tell you, either."

That's the funny thing about parenting. It's one catch-22 after another. While the no-tattle policy sounded like a good idea, it's not so nifty when it starts raining in the living room.

"Forget it," I announced.

"Are you sure?" he asked, smiling.

I nodded.

"Really?" he said happily. "Because guess what? Claire just took Mom's black bra across the street to show the neighbors."

Help!

There is, however, something worse than the kids tattling on each other—it's when they combine forces.

I don't know about your kids, but mine think an unsupervised kitchen is a playground for creating edible works of art without encumbering tools like paper towels, wash rags, and tarps.

Don't get me wrong, I am the first to encourage creativity . . . just not with sweet relish painted on a canvas of granola bars. My children are like Julia Child meets Pablo Picasso meets Oscar the Grouch.

Funny thing is, when my wife and I finally come downstairs, you'd think the children would have cleaned up, or at least blamed the dog, but they always seem surprised that anything is wrong. Somewhere along the line, didn't one of them turn to the other and say, "Nice melba toast and marshmallow sandwich. Now, we'd better clean up before Mom and Dad see this mess and slip into comas from the shock."

But they don't. Then, of course, I open my mouth and the dawn of realization spreads across their faces like two abstract artists seeing a rising mushroom cloud through the window of their paint-stained artist's loft.

Having been through this situation numerous times before (don't ask), I decided last weekend to first tour the operation like a true connoisseur of twenty-first-century food art before handing down my judgment.

"Hmmm, this looks interesting," I said. "What do you call it?"

"That's cherry pie filling rolled on graham cracker crumbs and served on a bed of crushed Oreos," my daughter explained. "It gave me a stomachache."

"Really? And this?"

"That's peanut butter stuffed inside a plum," my son answered. "But I'm not happy with it."

"Why not?"

"All the juice ran out when I hollowed out the middle."

"Well that certainly explains a lot," I replied.

"About what?"

"About why my stockinged feet are stuck to the kitchen floor."

"Yeah," my son retorted, "that happened to the cat, too. She's been under the couch ever since, licking her paws."

Finally, I lost it. "This is a disgrace! It looks like a pack of ferocious pirates ransacked the kitchen."

My son nodded. "Yeah, I think that's what happened."

I rolled my eyes. "Tell me you had a couple dozen friends over this time. Right? They were here watching cartoons with you—they made a couple collages with our condiments, maybe a mayonnaise finger-painting, and then went home to show their parents?"

My kids seemed perplexed. "No."

I looked around the kitchen another time. "So, is there anything left for Mom and I to eat for breakfast?"

"There's half a Pop-Tart on the windowsill," my daughter replied. "You might have to scrape a little mustard off, though."

After the kids were banished to their rooms, I turned to my wife. "So what happens when they are older and their creativity improves?"

"We quietly slip out of the house around midnight and rent our own apartment."

I can live with that.

I can live without eating in public with my children.

You know how it is when you go to a decent restaurant, one that costs a fair amount of money but you decided you and your family were worth it, and invariably, there's that one obnoxious family with the unruly children? The ones eating with their hands or shouting "Who cut the cheese?"

That's the Swarners.

I'd like to apologize.

Ironically, my wife and I are fairly reserved people who have really nice table manners. In fact, you could invite the two of us over to eat on your expensive wedding china and not feel the least bit uneasy.

The missus and I have also spent years training our children on proper manners. You'd think that would count for something. Of course, you'd also think my kids wouldn't grab the bread rolls before the server can finish placing the basket on our table.

Every time I think I've covered all the rules for eating out in public, my children prove me wrong. Who would have thought I'd need to go over the inappropriateness of drinking salad dressing with a straw?

I have, however, noticed you and your family while dining out. In fact, just the other day, I pointed out one of your children to my kids.

"Look at that child," I said. "You don't see him gulping milk, beating his knife like a drumstick, or diving under the table to demonstrate the earthquake drill he learned today at school."

"I'm not showing you what I did during the earthquake drill," my son argued.

I looked to the floor. "Then why are you under the table?"

"I dropped my roll."

"So what's taking you so long to get it?"

He stuck his head out from under the tablecloth. "I'm wiping the butter off your shoe."

Sometimes, I can't stand it any longer and I escape to the bathroom to sneak a few moments away from the carnage. Once inside, I can't tear myself away from the refreshing peace and tranquillity. Of course, I start to feel a little weird standing in there as people shuffle in and out, so to compensate, I pretend I'm a washroom attendant and hand paper towels to startled men exiting the toilet stalls.

Back at the table, I apologize to my wife for abandoning her and then I help sop up the spilled milk . . . in her purse.

The apologies don't end there. I also feel obliged to say sorry to our server. But he or she just usually laughs it off, explaining that it's really the busboy who will have to scrape the dried spaghetti sauce off the floor.

I half-expect to see my kids' faces on wanted posters the next time I walk into a restaurant. The sign will read: "Beware, wanted for food stains in 29 counties—considered armed and dangerous."

When I can no longer stand it (usually by dessert), I finally threaten my son and daughter. "I'm not taking you kids to a restaurant again," I yell. "Got that?!"

They typically nod sheepishly, even though they have that one memorized.

"Good," I'll add. "Now, on the count of three, everyone lift their feet for the busboy."

I've got to start eating at home more often!

I'll tell you, there is one thing I am doing for sure this year—I will be lobbying Congress asking for a national bedtime for all children.

I'm thinking 3 P.M., but I'm willing to negotiate.

My kids are fast approaching the age of discovery, and if an early bedtime decree is not established soon, one of their blabbermouth friends is going to tell them that our family's bedtime policy is not fair.

Already, there are rumblings at home.

"Jimmy says he stays up until 11 P.M.," my son told me.

"His parents have their own apartment over the garage?"

"No."

"Does Jimmy spend that time quietly in his room licking stamps or reading a book?"

"No."

I looked for eavesdroppers, then whispered: "Do his parents drink?"

"Huh?"

"Well something must be wrong with them," I proclaimed.

"All I know," my son said, "is that Jimmy stays up long enough to get dessert."

"You get dessert."

"Yeah, for breakfast."

So what happens when my son starts wondering what else Jimmy gets? See my dilemma? If all kids went to bed at the same time, who could complain?

"Son, the president declared a national bedtime today. You should feel proud—he chose yours." Then, I'll put my hands in the air and say, "Sorry, it's out of my control."

Early bedtime legislation won't be easy to pass. Fighting against it will be the kid's lobby, TV producers, and grandparents who don't want to play bad guy.

My mom has already given me grief about it.

"You put the kids to bed too early. Let them enjoy life."

"You should talk," I yelled. "Where do you think I came up with this idea?"

"I didn't make you go to bed that early when you were young."

"Then how come in high school I was voted most likely to wake up refreshed?"

It's not that I blame my mom for putting me to bed early. I'm not trying to get revenge. Now that I'm a dad, I know exactly why my mom did what she did. A strict bedtime is less for the children's well-being and everything for a mom and dad's sanity. Think of all the things you'd have time to do if the wee ones are in bed early: take piano lessons, read a book, call a friend, find those keys your kids buried in the backyard.

But you can kiss that freedom away if your neighbors aren't willing to play along—if they let Junior manage his own bedtime.

If you see my bill before Congress, please call and pledge your support. After all, such a law could only be the beginning. If it passed, next we could lobby for a national cap on allowances, a legal limit on the number of inane questions asked, and just maybe, a new amendment granting parents the right to choose their kids' friends.

Finally, I'd like to say that I am the quintessential pushover when it comes to busting a liar. My kids could be holding an armload of matches, tell me they didn't start the brushfire out back, and I'd believe them.

My wife, on the other hand, knows when my kids are fibbing even if they are just thinking it.

So, to help others in my situation catch their kids in the act, I have done a little lying research. Here are the basic things to look for:

1. **The Obvious Liar.** This little sneak will tell you he didn't give the dog a haircut even though he's standing there looking innocent, while not only holding the scissors, but also a little piece of puppy ear flesh. Poised there in his muddy boots, he'll deny he owns the footprints in the hall, on the stairs, and on your side of the bed. He says it wasn't him who tore his jeans or wet his pants.

When you ask who knocked over the doll case in the hallway, he'll ask "What doll case?"—even though he's pinned underneath it.

2. **The Blaming Liar.** This little sneak will tell you it's your fault she broke the lamp because you didn't tell her she shouldn't play dodgeball in the living room (you only said football). If she's caught cussing on the playground, she'll say she thought that word was okay because she heard it on TV, from the big kid next door, and when Grandpa put up the Christmas lights last December. She claims it's not her fault that she spilled paint on your car, opened your mail, or told her grandma that she looks like Uncle Jim. And when you ask her why she hit her little sister, she'll say an angel came to her in a dream and said, "Go forth, thy servant of God, and whap your sister upside the head."

3. **The Dumb Liar.** This little sneak will claim he was three blocks away at a friend's house when the towel rack came off the wall, even though that particular friend moved two months ago. If he forgets to call home, he'll tell you his friend doesn't have a phone, and if you don't believe him, you can call the friend's mother and she'll tell you. He'll tell you he didn't get his report card (even though his sister did), he'll say Mom ate the last piece of chicken (even though she's a vegetarian), and he'll blame the cat for knocking over the milk carton (even though Muffy has been dead for three years). And when you ask who left snot all over the lawn furniture, he'll say little Nicky next door did it, even

though he's only two and is known throughout the entire neighborhood to eat all of his boogers.

4. **The Clever Liar.** This little sneak is the worst because she'll actually fool one or both parents, getting away with all kinds of activities. If she has pinned her little brother on the floor and is forcing him to lick a doggie biscuit, just as you are rounding the corner, she'll flip the younger one on top of her, claiming the little brother started it. When caught red-handed with an off-limits cookie, she'll say Dad is mowing the lawn and wanted a Fig Newton. And when the car suspiciously rolls down the driveway and into the neighbor's mailbox, she'll tell you it narrowly missed her on her bike and aren't you relieved she wasn't crushed under the tires? (Through tears you will beg for her forgiveness.)

Sometime after she moves out, probably when she's twenty-six, she'll admit that after she made her brother lick the biscuit, she was actually in the car eating the Fig Newtons when she released the parking brake to see what would happen.

With all that said, you can imagine my recent trip to the analyst. It went something like this:

"Doctor, lately I have been feeling rather insecure as a parent."

"Go on."

"My kids yell in libraries," I explained. "When the glue runs out in the house, they substitute blue, tarter control toothpaste for it. They often forget to say thank you. I feel like I'm the only parent with imperfect children."

"How come?"

"Because most of my co-workers say so."

"They tell you that?"

"Well," I stammered, "they don't dispute it. For example, last month, I told Delores in Marketing that my kids ripped their towel rack off the wall again."

"Again?"

"Yeah. After I fixed it the first time, I told them no more hanging from the bar, but apparently they didn't think I also meant no fastening the cat to it."

"They fastened . . . ?"

"With duct tape. Anyway, I thought Delores would empathize with me, or share a similar story about her kids, or say she'd keep an eye out for a runaway cat wandering the streets with a towel bar taped to its face, but she just stared at me in horror and said her children would never DREAM of doing something like that."

The doctor smiled. "And you're worried about that?"

"Not at first," I replied. "I shrugged it off, but later decided to bring up the story at lunch to see what other parents had to say."

"And?"

"Well, one person said her daughter loves her cat, another wanted to know my kids' names so she could pray for us, and Terry in Purchasing just sat quietly and wept."

"Go on."

"So, two weeks ago I started lying."

"Lying?"

"Uh-huh. I decided I would no longer tell anyone the awful things my children did, and, instead, I'd pretend they were my little angels."

"Has that worked?" he asked.

"Most of the time," I replied. "Of course, a few people overheard me talking on the phone with the school principal the other day."

The doctor looked over his clipboard. "What was that all about?"

I cleared my throat. "My little seven-year-old cussed on the playground."

"How did that go over with your staff?"

"It was tense," I admitted. "But I think I smoothed things over when I told everyone in the break room that it's probably because my daughter's Brownie troop volunteers at the prison. The only problem is, yesterday, I started seriously questioning my lies."

"Why?"

"Well, a new-hire came up to me all upset and asked when my son was out of diapers."

The doctor made a notation. "What did you say?"

I blanched. "I told her that my son was potty trained at one and a half—and in fact, by two he was scolding me for leaving the empty toilet paper tube on the spindle."

"Did you feel better?"

"Sure, then her eyes started to puff up and she cried. I felt awful, so I backtracked and told her the truth—that my son was four before he was in underwear, and it will probably be a cold day in hell before he ever learns to flush a toilet."

"What did she say?"

"She said. 'Oh, thank God, Ken, I was really worried. My

son was out of diapers at two and a half—I thought there was something wrong with him.'"

The doctor stared blankly.

I sighed. "Why is it always you and me, Doc, with the imperfect kids?"

The room was silent.

"Your kids aren't perfect, are they?" I asked. "Why aren't you saying anything?"

12

Didn't I Already Graduate?

"I promised myself a good stiff belt of vanilla if I lived through this morning."

—Erma Bombeck

Philosophers say that life is a continuing education class. I think this is especially true when your children are in elementary school. Since the day my cherubs started kindergarten, I've learned humility, patience, and the phone number of a good shrink. I've also done some extra credit and discovered:

1. Teachers know if you do your daughter's homework.

2. If you forget to send money to school for a field trip, your child will invariably say quite innocently and in a loud voice: "I'm not sure my parents can afford it."

3. When laundry is low and you dress your child in an outfit that doesn't exactly match—that's picture day.

I suppose my crowning moment so far is the following exchange of letters that took place last year:

MONDAY:
Dear Mr. Swarner,
Alasdair said he forgot his lunch today, but this afternoon I found his lunchbox buried under our dried noodle collages. When I asked him why he did this, he said he couldn't face another peanut butter sandwich, bag of chips, and piece of stale Halloween candy. Do you think he feels insecure about his nourishment?
Sincerely yours, Alasdair's teacher,
Ms. Goodesteem

TUESDAY
Dear Ms. Goodesteem,
Both my wife and I work, so gourmet lunch-making is quite a luxury (as is grocery shopping). I would like to point out, however, that the candy was a Blow Pop.
Respectively yours, Alasdair's father,
Ken Swarner

TUESDAY:
Dear Mr. Swarner,
The BLT seemed to pick up your son's spirits today. Have you and your wife tried sharing the lunch-making duties? You do the sandwiches, and she chops the fruit? P.S. It warms my heart to see a child interacting positively with his meal.
Yours truly,
Ms. Goodesteem

WEDNESDAY:

Goodesteem,

That wasn't a BLT. Try bacon, lettuce, and Cheetos (we
were all out of anything red). Thanks for the advice, but my
wife and I have almost divorced over lunches. Our coun-
selor Peggy helped us compromise: I make the lunches, and
my wife does everything else (which still gives me the raw
end of the stick). Long live Skippy.

Mr. Swarner

WEDNESDAY:

Dear Mr. Swarner,

I think we are slipping back into some bad habits. Your son
had the same old sandwich again. Why don't we try what
some of my other parents do: Tomorrow morning, wake up
an extra 30 minutes early and cook your son a bowl of
spaghetti or ravioli for lunch. You could butter a few slices
of bread and toss a small green salad. Think how special
that would be for him.

Sincerely yours,

Ms. Goodesteem

THURSDAY:

Teacher,

Spaghetti? Getting up early? Maybe you wish to see me
have a nervous breakdown—the kind where I quit work and
sit on my front porch all day wearing only light blue pajama
bottoms? You don't have children, do you?

Mr. Swarner

THURSDAY:

Mr. Swarner,

Ms. Goodesteem was not suggesting that you wear anything on your porch. She is just concerned with your son's nutrition. There are many easy lunches that would offer your child variety, like my favorite: olive loaf.

Signed, Alasdair's principal,

Ms. Gloria Winterbottom

FRIDAY:

Ms. Winterbottom,

Maybe I haven't been clear enough. My morning starts out with scrounging for breakfast because all the milk is gone. Then, there is usually a daily challenge, like finding my son's homework in the recycle bin, or pulling my daughter's shoe out of the heating duct. After this, I make the lunches in assembly row fashion. Switching to lunch meat would require concentration that I usually reserve for driving to school in rush hour traffic while the children sing "Jingle Bells, Batman Smells" at the top of their lungs. Thanks for the advice; it's nice to know you care.

Swarner

FRIDAY

Mr. Swarner,

I have only one reply: Buy lunch!

Winterbottom

After Lamaze, day care is the first hurdle along the path as most parents embark on the road of education. Day care is a lot like elementary school—the only difference being instead of bringing glue and number two pencils, you bring diapers and a spit rag.

In the beginning, it is a relatively easy process—you hand off the baby, then return eight hours later and pick him up—sort of like dry cleaning.

Eventually, however, the child grows a little older and comes under the impression that if he played his cards right, he could stay with you all day rather than going to day care. These are dangerous thoughts that kids learn on the playground from big kids.

When the child realizes, however, that she is going to day care and not spending the day playing with Play-Doh in your cubicle, all hell breaks loose.

Life is never quite the same for parents afterward. You spend the rest of your days feeling guilty for every time you dropped him off in the morning and he cried, whined, or pulled so hard on your arm it dislocated your shoulder.

In my case, I didn't have a warning for this switch in the tides. One day I was dropping off my son with the day care staff he loved and adored, and the next day, he acted like he had never seen these people before.

The morning of this first fit had started well enough. He had no problem putting away his coat, and aside from throwing one of his shoes at his nap partner, everything seemed routine . . . until, as I was leaving, he grabbed my neck and screamed: "DADDY, DON'T LEAVE ME!" He might have well said, "DADDY, DON'T KILL ME!" I felt terrible.

Other veteran parents rushing in to drop off their kids stopped for a moment and stared at me in silence as if I was a war memorial. One dad, who obviously had older kids, put his hand over his heart and looked close to tears.

I, on the other hand, was turning blue.

Finally, one of the day care staff rushed over and took my child so I could breathe. That was a relief, until my son did a wet noodle, hit the ground, and ran full force into my bad knee.

Checking my watch, I decided I could afford an extra five minutes, so I limped over to the plush toys for a quiet pow-wow with my boy.

"Son," I said, "what happened? You used to be excited to learn new things and meet new kids. Remember?"

He nodded.

"So Daddy can go to work now?"

He nodded again.

Satisfied, I stood up and started to walk away with him holding on to my tie—he got a rug burn on his knees.

Sitting back down, I noticed for the first time another dad sitting on a beanbag a few feet away wearing a wrinkled suit and a crown of Tinker Toys. His daughter sat guard at his feet working on a puzzle.

He leaned over and handed me his business card. "If you get to the outside, please tell my boss to donate my cubicle to someone needy," he said.

Determined to leave, I picked up my child and walked to the entrance. "Son," I said, "I love you. You are going to have a wonderful day. Daddy will see you this afternoon." I placed him in the loving vise-grip of the center's owner and gave him a kiss.

I walked to my car listening to his bloodcurdling screams echo in the still morning air. Hopping into my seat, I was afraid to look back at him. I wasn't sure my heart could handle seeing him reaching out to me as if I had just given him up for adoption. I drew in a deep breath and sneaked a peek.

Surprisingly, he wasn't crying. In fact, he was jumping up

and down excited, waving something back and forth. "Whew," I exclaimed waving back. "That's not so bad. No reason to feel guilty." Then my stomach churned as I realized that my son was holding my briefcase. The day care worker, standing next to him, was motioning me back inside.

As I walked to the entrance, I wondered how long it was until naptime, and in the meantime, maybe the other dad would be up for a game of Monopoly.

Aside from the above, I think picking a day care rings true as my worst experience of parenthood . . . so far.

I was at the YMCA one day when a dad told an expectant father in the locker room that all day cares are the same.

I practically fell out of my towel when I heard this. I assume Mr. Ill-Informed has had the good fortune to need only one childcare provider for his family. But take it from me: I've had my kids in three, and they were nothing alike.

Our first day care was a disaster. We left that place after they called me in the middle of the day with alarming news.

"Mr. Swarner, something's wrong with your son!"

"What happened?" I asked shaking. "Is he breathing? Wait! I'll be right over."

When I arrived they brought me into the owner's office and asked me to sit down. The staff stared at their feet nervously.

"Coffee, Mr. Swarner?"

"Look," I said. "It's best you just tell me what happened. Where's my son?"

The owner paused a second and then spoke: "Your son spit up."

My face sank. "Blood?"

"No, peas," she said. "Now you shouldn't panic, but he should see a doctor, and we'd like him to stay home until he can act normal."

"He's eight months," I said.

"It shot out of his mouth like confetti, Mr. Swarner . . . it scared the latch-key kids."

We checked out that day.

The next day care we chose for our son was worse. They didn't care if my child spit up, nor how long it stayed on his shirt. We'd send our kids there with spotless clothes and faces, and they'd return looking like victims of a fraternity food fight. We asked the day care to use the bibs we sent, but that didn't keep the peanut butter and jelly off our kids' shoes.

I finally gave up and dressed my children in dry-cleaner bags.

Enter our present day care—the land of milk and honey, not to mention a center with clean floors, educational programs, and employees who don't use the word *sucks*.

Chatting with friends, I can safely say my journey to find decent childcare has not been unique. And for some, it is still the eternal quest. But, borrowing from their and my experiences, if I had to write it down, I'd have to say a good day care:

1. Doesn't expect you to do their job for them, but actually takes care of your children—heating their lunch, cleaning them up, and taking sharp objects out of their hands.

2. Doesn't call you at work because your daughter has a sniffle, which "might" develop into something serious, but waits until she actually throws up on her nap partner before dragging you out of a staff meeting.

3. Doesn't laugh at your wrinkled clothes, hair sticking up, and mismatched socks as you frantically

rush your child into the center each morning. They just hand you a doughnut and call your employer to say you'll be late.

4. Doesn't focus on the times your son ran through the center with his clothes off, but instead, tells you proudly about "his consistent stools and outstanding appetite."

5. Doesn't tell you about his first steps, first words, first burp, or first dry nap, but leads you to BELIEVE that all of his firsts miraculously happened either in the evening or on the weekend when you were luckily around to see them.

Eventually, however, day care ends as kids grow older and lifestyles change.

For all the hassles, I'll miss day care, though, because in many ways, it's an integral part of my life experience. As I sat down to write this book, I started thinking about my favorite memories of the day care years—wondering if they, in some twisted way, mirror those memories of others. Here are my favorite four day care experiences:

1. Sitting at the dinner table one evening when my son stopped playing with his food and said: "I told my day care teacher that Grandma is going to stay with us this summer."

   "That's nice," my wife answered.

   "And that Daddy said he's going to buy a great big dog to bite her if she tries to get out of her room."

   (I was joking.)

2. Receiving this call from my mother: "Ken, I picked your daughter up at day care to go shopping for new clothes, only, she isn't wearing any underwear."

   "I could have sworn I put Batgirl panties on her this morning," I told my mom. Frustrated, I spent the next hour searching unsuccessfully for the underwear around the house. Later that evening, the mystery was solved when a parent called to say her son came home from day care . . . wearing them.

   (Where his Barney briefs are, no one knows still today.)

3. Discovering my daughter learned a new game at day care called "Sexy."

   "Yeah, Dad, it's really neat!" she explained. "You pull your shirt up like this and dance around singing, 'Sexy, I'm so sexy!'"

   My dinner guests were a little shocked to hear this, but I think I covered pretty well when I asked, "More dessert, anyone?"

4. Our final day of day care before the kids started elementary school. My wife, our children, and myself stood in the center, thanking the staff for all of their support. Later, as we were heading for the door, my daughter shouted really loud, "See Daddy, we are all done with day care and you were wrong—it didn't cost us our arms and legs. We still have them!"

Yep—lots of good memories (gulp!).

During the Halloween of my son's preschool year, I made a mistake of epic proportions. He brought home a jack-o-lantern picture he made at day care, and I acted as if it should hang in the New York Museum of Modern Art as the quintessential example of late-twentieth-century finger-painting. I went out and bought special refrigerator magnets and a frame. I showed it to everyone who dropped by for a visit.

Little did I know at the time, however, as I made my son stand by his painting so I could snap a picture for Grandma, that I was fast approaching a period when art would flow home from school like lava from an erupting volcano. The problem here was my reinforcing message to my son that every art project deserved a special showing. The other problem was that my wife agreed. So, after he and his sister entered elementary school, my refrigerator was immediately plastered with art from corner to corner. There were so many pictures on it that ten magnets fell to my feet every time I opened the door.

Next, I tacked the crafts to the walls, placed the heavier stuff on tables, and once, when no one was looking, I fed the dog a macaroni necklace. After all of that, I figured I would either have to buy a bigger house, or find somewhere else for the crafts to go. It's not like I could throw the art in the garbage. There's nothing sadder than an art project in the garbage—unless it's a sobbing first-grader digging her art project out of the garbage.

That's when I started taking the art to work and throwing it into the garbage. Only, before long, I started to feel guilty about that—especially when I saw a garbage truck pass by with my daughter's pilgrim puppet attached to its antenna.

With nowhere else to turn, I decided to decorate my office at work with the art. Eventually, I ran out of room there, too—so I tried farming the art projects out to my co-workers. I took Joe in Accounting a yarn-wrapped paper clip holder, but he already had three. I tried to give Ellen a Christmas paperweight, but she had thrown her back out carrying the "Plymouth Rock" her son made for her. I did, however, get lucky and pawned a turkey my daughter traced with her hand to Marge whose only son went away to college this year. She cried.

Despite the challenges, I can at least feel good that my kids are proud every time they walk into my office. After all, it looks like Romper Room.

My boss, on the other hand, isn't so sure. He stopped by the other day.

"Who are you looking for?" I asked him as he stood searching my cubicle with a funny look on his face.

He blinked. "Captain Kangaroo."

If the schools continue with the art projects, I think I'm going to have to rent a storage unit . . . or maybe start decorating the inside of my car.

If you'd like one—please let me know.

And speaking of crafts, here's one of my favorite holiday songs:

The Twelve Days of Crafts

On the first day of Christmas, my firstborn gave to me, a picture of a pear tree.

On the second day of Christmas, my firstborn gave to me, two homemade ties and a picture of a pear tree.

On the third day of Christmas, my firstborn gave to me, three handprints, two homemade ties, and a picture of a pear tree.

On the fourth day of Christmas, my firstborn gave to me, four glitter balls, three handprints, two homemade ties, and a picture of a pear tree.

On the fifth day of Christmas, my firstborn gave to me, five tie-dyed shirts, four glitter balls, three handprints, two homemade ties, and a picture of a pear tree.

On the sixth day of Christmas, my firstborn gave to me, six rings of twisties, five tie-dyed shirts, four glitter balls, three handprints, two homemade ties, and a picture of a pear tree.

On the seventh day of Christmas, my firstborn gave to me, seven rocks a-painted, six rings of twisties, five tie-dyed shirts, four glitter balls, three handprints, two homemade ties, and a picture of a pear tree.

On the eighth day of Christmas, my firstborn gave to me, eight strings of Fruit Loops, seven rocks a-painted, six rings of twisties, five tie-dyed shirts, four glitter balls, three handprints, two homemade ties, and a picture of a pear tree.

On the ninth day of Christmas, my firstborn gave to me, nine crayon drawings, eight strings of Fruit Loops, seven rocks a-painted, six rings of twisties, five tie-dyed shirts, four glitter balls, three handprints, two homemade ties, and a picture of a pear tree.

On the tenth day of Christmas, my firstborn gave to me, ten pots with glazing, nine crayon drawings, eight strings of Fruit Loops, seven rocks a-painted, six rings of twisties, five tie-dyed shirts, four glitter balls, three handprints, two homemade ties, and a picture of a pear tree.

On the eleventh day of Christmas, my firstborn gave to me, eleven noodle collages, ten pots with glazing, nine crayon drawings, eight strings of Fruit Loops, seven rocks a-painted, six rings of twisties, five tie-dyed shirts, four glitter balls, three handprints, two homemade ties, and a picture of a pear tree.

On the twelfth day of Christmas, my firstborn gave to me, twelve cotton snowmen, eleven noodle collages, ten pots with glazing, nine crayon drawings, eight strings of Fruit Loops, seven rocks a-painted, six rings of twisties, five tie-dyed shirts, four glitter balls, three handprints, two home-made ties, and (big finish) a picture of a pear tree.

I knew something was wrong when I picked up my son at school and I saw one of his classmates carrying a large cardboard display with pictures and words out to her parent's car.

I turned around and looked at my son in the backseat. "Are you working on reports in school?"

He nodded sheepishly.

"What is yours about?"

"The Iroquois Indians."

"Why haven't I heard anything about it?" I asked suspiciously. "Is it a big project?"

He handed me the directions from the teacher—they were, oh, two pages.

"What have you done so far?"

"I've made an Indian headdress."

"Really," I said. "How?"

"Well, I was going to find bird feathers in the backyard and weave them into a leather band," he explained, "but it was too hard."

"So?"

"So, I took feathers from your pillow and glued them to Mom's hairclip."

I stared in shock. "When is your report due?"

"Tomorrow."

"What!? And all you have is a hair accessory? How do you plan to get all twelve of these requirements on the directions done by tomorrow?"

"I was going to ask you for help," he replied, looking perfectly calm.

"Just me," I asked, "or did you also plan to enlist the neighbors to help out?"

"Do you think they would?"

"Of course," I answered. "I'm sure the Army colonel next door would love to come over and make little Sacagawea finger-puppets out of toilet paper tubes."

"Dad, Sacagawea wasn't an Iroquois."

"Good, you know that, huh? So at the very least, you can write that on a sticky note and turn it in with the hairclip."

When we got home, I sent him upstairs with cardboard poster paper to make his display. Later, I walked into his room, expecting to find him hard at work. Instead, he was wadding up his clean underwear and shooting baskets into the trash can.

I held my anger. Instead, I pointed out that this assignment was his project, and it wasn't my responsibility to make sure he was on task. He promised to do his report, and by the look on his face, I believed him . . . until he and his sister slid down the stairs on the cardboard display.

I finally lost it. "You're going to fail at this rate!" I yelled as I taped the tear in the cardboard. "Don't expect me to stay up all night helping you!"

Around 1 A.M., my wife stepped drowsily into the dining room where I was pasting down block lettering on the Iroquois project.

"How's it going?" she asked.

"I'm beat," I said, rubbing my eyes.

"Where's your son?"

"Asleep under the chair with the cat."

She looked around the table. "Is that my hairclip over there?"

I nodded. "It goes with the Indian mask I made with your ski hat."

"So," she continued, "did your son learn a lesson in all of this?"

"Of course," I replied. "He learned that his dad is a sucker."

Speaking of suckers, when the invitation arrived home it seemed innocent enough. My daughter's teacher was looking for parents to volunteer for the upcoming Thanksgiving Day lunch. My daughter asked me to come, so, naturally, I signed up. After all, I thought, how hard could it be to help serve twenty-two third-graders some turkey and mashed potatoes?

From here on out, I need to remind myself that when I say "How hard could it be?" there is probably a reason I'm saying that.

The party was a reenactment in the school library of the first Thanksgiving. The children made place mats, colored decorations, prepared the food, and dressed up in order to provide a certain sense of realism to the celebration.

I arrived a few minutes late but just in time to see Captain Standish hit Priscilla with a dictionary. While they marched to the principal's office, I helped chase the kids off the buffet table and tried to curb the potty talk in the hand-washing lines. Then, when the children were threatened to take their seats or not eat, my daughter's teacher, Ms. Feelgood, held up a large, brown, paper hat and asked: "Which parent wants to wear the pilgrim hat and carve the turkey?"

The room fell silent for a moment. One parent quietly slipped out to the bathroom, another one grabbed a book and pretended to read, a third said she had a rare follicle disease, and a forth ran screaming out of the building.

"I guess you're it, Mr. Swarner," the teacher exclaimed.

The children clapped with glee, shouting "Mr. Swarner" over and over. I suppose I would have enjoyed the positive reception if the staples holding the hat together hadn't scratched my ears as Ms. Feelgood slammed the thing down over my head.

"How's that?" she asked me.

"Fine," I replied. "Did pilgrims happen to have Band-Aids?"

Ms. Feelgood handed me a large fork and carving knife.

My dad always cuts the Thanksgiving turkey in our family, so I gulped as I walked apprehensively over to the golden brown bird. It looked delicious sitting there on a large platter garnished with parsley and vegetables. By the time I was done carving it, however, it reminded me of roadkill.

"I'm not very good at this," I explained nervously to the other parents.

"I can see that," one mother retorted. "Is there any white meat, or is all of it marbled now?"

I helped dish up the children's plates and then I took my seat next to my daughter. As I sat down in the little elementary chair, my knees pressed up hard against my chest. "Are you okay, Daddy?" my little girl asked.

"I think so," I gasped. "Why do you ask?"

"Because you're wheezing."

The lunch was delicious. Bowls passed back and forth as we all enjoyed the food the children made. As the feast progressed, the children talked excitedly with their mouths full about school, recess, and friends.

Then, a boy named Reggie leaned into my space.

"Mr. Swarner?"

"Yes," I replied.

"That cranberry sauce makes a funny pattern on your teeth," Reggie said. "When you talk, it looks like your mouth is bleeding."

"Thanks for noticing," I retorted. "Anything else?"

"Yes—can you face the other direction—it's grossing me out."

I excused myself to the bathroom and brushed my teeth with my finger. When I returned, the kids had been excused to recess. It took thirty minutes to pick the dropped food out of the carpet. By the time I returned to work, I was exhausted.

Later that night, when my daughter was telling my wife how the party went, I realized something.

"And then Daddy wore the funny pilgrim hat, and someone said his teeth were bleeding but it was really his ears, and then Ms. Feelgood and another mom had to help him out of his chair because he was stuck . . ."

While my little girl told her mom these things, she looked at me as if I had done something extremely heroic by simply showing up.

Maybe I did.

Yesterday I signed up for the Christmas party.

13

For Better or for Worse

"In every house of marriage there's room for an interpreter."
—Stanley Kunitz

Notes left by two working parents:

MONDAY:
Sweetheart,
It's Claire's turn to bring snack to school today. There's celery in the fridge. Cut it up into two-inch chunks, spread peanut butter on them, and place five raisins on each. Wrap in cellophane (not a dry cleaners bag!), and be sure there are twenty-four plus one for her teacher, Ms. Feelgood. Tidy the family room if you get a chance. Did you call the plumber yet?
I love you,
Allison

MONDAY:
Honey,
That was okra, not celery. Claire saw me spreading Cheez

Whiz on them and cried for twenty minutes until I forked over twenty-four pieces of Halloween candy (who told the kids the candy was hidden in the vacuum bag?). By the time I untied your son's double knots with your graduation pen, the family room was a lost cause. Dinner is on time bake. I have Rotary tonight. Was the pen important?

Hugs and kisses,

Ken

TUESDAY:

Ken,

The toilet has been asking for the plumber. You forgot Alasdair's milk money again. He says he owes some fifth grader $3.25 plus interest for milk loans. I have a meeting tonight. The mess has spread to the dining room.

Love,

Allison

TUESDAY:

Allison,

I couldn't find Alasdair's lunchbox so I used your hat. Call the principal about the loan shark. Replaced your graduation pen—disregard the year. I think you took my car keys this morning—the taxi's here, got to go.

Sincerely,

Ken

WEDNESDAY:

Hey,

Your keys were in the juice pitcher. The kids won't go to the bathroom—when's the plumber coming? I enjoyed our talk last night. We have to abandon the downstairs to the clutter

and take refuge upstairs tonight. Dinner is on your son's top
bunk.
Allison

WEDNESDAY:

Al,

We didn't have a conversation last night—our bed was full
of kids; I slept with the dog. What's the plumber's phone
number? Did you know Tuesday was class picture day, and
your son wore his "I'm with stupid" T-shirt? Apparently he
stood next to his teacher.

Ken

THURSDAY:

The neighbor called—something about your son and some
jumper cables. I said you'd stop by tonight and talk to her. I
spoke with the principal; picture retakes are next Monday . . .
I burned the shirt. We owe the principal $4.50 for loaning
our son milk money, too.

A.

THURSDAY:

Yesterday was Alasdair's snack day. Luckily, I had gum. I
promise I'll call the plumber today.

K.

FRIDAY:

Wife,

I had a breakfast meeting this morning. I sandbagged the
bathroom last night; call the National Guard if it crests.
Any idea where the cat is?

Me

FRIDAY:

Husband,

Provisions are low, and something is moving in the living room . . . could be the cat. Order pizza and watch out for the waterfall on the stairs.

P.S. Bring your sleeping bag; we're in the attic divvying up the rest of the Halloween candy.

My wife and I were the first among our friends to have children.

Two toddlers later, my wife sat me down one day with an invitation in her hand. "Ken, we've been invited to the Pierce's barbecue."

"Great!" I exclaimed. "But why the sullen face?"

"I don't know exactly how to say this," she said cautiously.

"Then just say it."

"At parties, you talk too much about the kids—people can't relate."

I did a double take. "Me? Look whose talking, miss 'I think I'll mention how many diapers I changed this year in the Christmas letter.'"

"People like statistics," she retorted.

"It gave my mom the willies," I exclaimed. "I think you violated a couple postal laws, too."

"Okay," she replied. "Maybe we both have a problem. Let's just try to go to one party without coming off like Mike and Carol Brady. Okay?"

I nodded.

A week later, we walked into the party with plenty else to talk about. I planned to steer conversations toward baseball and my wife was ready to discuss popular music. We were set.

I was minding my own business at the buffet table when my

good friend Bob asked me to pass the honey for his corn muffin. Before I knew what I was doing, I spent ten minutes explaining why babies can't eat honey.

"Let's just say there's very little Ho Ho Ho with diarrhea on Christmas Day."

As Bob wandered off looking pale, I glanced nervously around for my wife, but luckily, she was across the room talking with friends and didn't hear me. Okay, it was only a little slipup, I reassured myself, just before I grabbed up a tortilla and showed the Pierce's parents how I can diaper with only one hand.

Feeling guilty, I moved away from the food and stood with my back against the living room wall trying to remain inconspicuous. Before I could stop him, my old college roommate, Phil, approached and asked me, "Have you done anything exciting, lately, Ken?"

"I rescued a marble from my son's nose," I answered automatically, kicking myself the moment I said it.

His face contorted. "Really?"

"Yeah, I pinched right between the poor kid's eyes and it popped out like a bloody cannonball."

He stood looking shocked.

I lowered my voice, "The doctor said he'll probably have uneven nostrils until Easter."

Dang! I yelled at myself, checking once again to make sure my wife didn't hear. Sure enough, she was across the room chatting effortlessly, I figured, about something—probably music or wine or anything exclusively adultlike.

Disgusted, I pantomimed a ticker-lock for my mouth and moved into the next room. I sat quietly for a long time, but, just as I was about to get up, a woman I hadn't met before sat down next to me.

"Are you having a good time?" I asked her.

"Sure," she smiled. "Everyone seems really nice, except of course, for that crazy woman demonstrating her labor to everyone."

"Which woman?"

"There," she said, pointing into the next room at my wife, who at that moment was putting a sofa pillow up her dress.

"You mean the one breathing really loud?" I asked.

She nodded. "Time to toss out that pillow."

Later, as my wife and I drove home, she turned to me, "Do you think we'll ever be invited back?"

"Sure," I answered. "As soon as they can get the image out of their heads of you delivering a healthy baby pillow."

That story is a fine example of how closely knitted my wife and I really are—how we often have the same issues and see eye to eye on subjects.

Except for the times we don't. Like when my wife announced it was time to have another baby. She said she missed having an infant around the house, so it is time to bring one more Swarner into the world.

I found her speech very interesting to hear because I was pretty sure she knew that I had had a vasectomy. After all, she took me to the doctor. She drove me home. She brought me little sips of water while I laid on the couch all weekend wearing an athletic supporter and asking Jesus for mercy.

"These things can be undone," she told me.

"Undone?" I replied. "Are we talking about the same thing here? You sound like you're talking about a haircut!"

"Lots of guys are having reverses," she announced.

"Is that what it's called?" I asked. "You'd think they'd call it a crisis."

"Honey, it's a standard procedure. It's not major surgery."

"I'm not worried about the surgery."

"What then?"

"Gravity—mostly. Oh, and walking with a permanent limp."

She smiled reassuringly. "I am sure you'll be doing things like playing tennis before you know it."

"Gosh, you're probably right," I answered. "I suppose I might need help putting on my tennis shorts, or I might need someone to hold a tennis racquet between my teeth while I work through the pain, but I'm sure plenty of people at the tennis club are familiar with those sorts of things."

She shook her head at me.

I continued. "So, how is this done?"

She explained the procedure. Apparently, the doctor reattaches the tiny vas (tubing that carries the sperm) that was originally cut apart and cauterized when I had my vasectomy by sewing the end pieces together with microscopic sutures.

"What if it doesn't work?" I asked her.

"No baby."

"But I have a thousand pieces of thread stitched down there?"

"Basically."

"So," I continued, "assuming it works, what happens the next time we are done having kids? Another vasectomy? Then, you change your mind again, and another reversal, followed by a vasectomy? Eventually, won't I be out of sperm tubing?"

"I don't know."

"You don't know?" I asked incredulously. "Sweetheart, I've seen you labor for hours making Halloween costumes every year. I've seen you spend days contemplating Easter outfits for the kids. Don't you think you ought to closely consider the pattern here before some seamstress with a medical degree hems my vas?"

My wife smiled. "If you run out, maybe you could get a transplant."

"Is that now on the organ donor cards?"

She turned and walked away.

"Where are you going?" I shouted after her.

"To call the doctor and make an appointment for you," she answered. "I read somewhere that you should never put off to tomorrow what you can do today."

Funny, but at that moment I was thinking the very same thing . . . in regards to running away from home, that is.

While I am not looking forward to such an operation, my wife is dreading the next time something breaks in our house. Although my wife wouldn't trade me in for a movie star, a doctor, a lawyer, a lion tamer (for kids) or, for that matter, a better listener, a feminist, or someone who can spit out toothpaste directly into the drain, she just might one day trade me for a handyman.

I can change a tire. I can dig a ditch. But purposefully removing the plate from a light switch is hair loss and three days at the general hospital waiting to happen. Some guys were raised on a farm or had a lot of leaky faucets out in the middle of nowhere and they know their way around a circular saw or electric sander. I, on the other hand, grew up in the suburbs—my most handy tool is the cordless Yellow Pages.

I started thinking about this the other day when my neighbor Terry the Toolman was outside demonstrating to his son how to build a seventeen-story high-rise birdhouse while I was inside showing my boy how to open a bag of Fritos. "Grab both ends carefully son, and pull."

It's not that I'm afraid of tools. My wife bought me a set last Christmas, and they have been quite useful: A screwdriver keeps the garage door shut, a hammer is holding a pile of newspapers in place, and the kids have strung bolts into trendy necklaces and should have sold enough at school soon to send us all to Hawaii.

My wife is disappointed. "Aren't all men supposed to be handy?"

"We have hands, yes," I answered.

"You know what I mean. Women cook," she said.

"I cook."

"Women clean."

"I clean. Are you saying if I were a handyman I wouldn't have to cook dinners and help clean the house?" I asked.

"Never mind."

However, she doesn't like imposing on her father all the time.

"Then why don't we hire someone?" I suggested.

"When my dad does it for free? I just wish YOU could do it."

That's when I start talking about punching a hole in the wall to re-route a wire and my wife calls her dad.

"Ken, go find me a crescent wrench," my father-in-law asked me recently when he stopped by to fix the dishwasher after the kids used it to re-create Noah's Ark.

I scurried off.

"Did you find it?" he asked.

"I'm not sure!" I shouted down the hall. "It might be holding the bunkbeds together or I might have used it as a Christmas ornament."

"It's right here," he said fishing it out of a drawer.

"Oh, the meat tenderizer. So, what's wrong?"

"Well," he said rubbing his chin. "We're going to have to punch a hole in the wall and re-route some wires."

My wife's face snapped to attention.

That lucky guess should keep her from trading me in for at least another year.

Of course, marriage is a two-way street, and I certainly have my share of road bumps to navigate. Like the last time she and I stuffed ourselves at a dinner party. The next day, she announced "I am going to lose weight."

"I know," I replied.

She knitted her eyebrows. "What do you mean, *you know?* I just decided right now."

I grinned. "Honey, every few months you resolve to lose weight—you've been doing it since 1991."

"That may be so, but this time, I am hiring help."

"A personal trainer?" I asked.

"No."

"Dietician?"

"No."

"Who?"

"You."

"Me?"

"Yes, I want you to help me," she exclaimed. "I want your support."

"I can't," I replied. "I get light-headed when I diet."

"No, I want you to stop me from eating things I shouldn't."

"How?"

"I want you to say something."

"Like what?" I asked.

"Like, 'Drop the cookie before you can't fit through the front door.'"

I did a double take. "I'm supposed to do that every time you try to eat a snack?"

"No. You could also make a pig noise."

"A what?"

"When I reach for a treat," she explained, "you squeal like a piggy."

"A pig?"

"Yes—oink, oink."

"Then what happens?"

"I'll probably cry, but you want to support me, don't you?"

I sat down. "So, let me get this straight—you want me to be your food cop?"

She nodded.

"And if the swine noises don't work, I'm supposed to . . ."

"Throw the book at me."

"What book?"

"This one," she said, holding up a copy of Dr. Sheila Gunderson's new self-help book, *You Eat Like a Hippo*.

"That doesn't sound nice," I exclaimed.

"Look, if I wanted nice, I'd call my mom so she can tell me AGAIN that my double chin is a sign of sincerity."

I sat thinking into space for a moment. "What happens if we are in public—like at a wedding or something?"

"I've thought about that," she replied. "And, very discreetly, I want you to push me down whenever I am within six feet of the buffet line."

"Wha? What if I'm on the other side of the room?"

"Well, then pay the wait staff to slap my hand every time I reach for a canapé."

There was something about this plan that just didn't sit right with me. "Honey, maybe we should think about this for a few days."

"We don't have to," she retorted. "I'm ready to go."

"This is all easy for you to say right now—especially after just finishing a heavy meal," I said. "But how are you going to feel come Valentine's Day when I have you pinned under my knee and I'm wrestling a Hershey Kiss from your grip? Do you really think this will be good for our marriage? And how's it going to look a few years from now on *Oprah* when she does 'The Awful Things Our Husband's Do' episode and you're imitating my pig snorts in front of a shocked studio audience?" I frowned. "Oprah's liable to take a swing at me for something like that."

My wife's eyes flashed. "What? Am I the only one willing to sacrifice here?"

Although this exchange might seem odd, it's actually quite normal for my wife. As was this following conversation:

"Honey," my wife called from beyond one Sunday afternoon.

I turned down the sound on the TV. "What?!" I yelled.

"Come here."

"You come here," I shouted.

Dead space. I turned the sound back up, sat staring at the screen blankly for several seconds, then threw the remote in disgust and trotted off to find her. "What?" I kept repeating, trying to hone in on her presence like a bat tracks fruit. "What? What? What?" Finally, I found her in her closet. "WHAT?!"

"Oh, there you are," she answered. "Do you like this dress?"

My knees suddenly went weak. I hate pop quizzes like this for three reasons: 1. The only right answer is the one she has already formulated in her mind. 2. No bell-curve averaging. 3. The short-answer portion of the test is usually followed by a grueling oral essay in which I, the testee, must supply to my wife, the tester, three main points and twenty-seven footnotes correlating to the answer I didn't want to give in the first place.

"It looks fine," was my response.

"Oh pleeeeez," she retorted.

"What?"

She shook her head. "You said that about the brown dress last week, the two-piece I wore to the 4th of July pool party, my apron two Thanksgivings ago, and the bedhead I had the day our nephew was circumcised."

"Is it my fault you look good in everything?" I yelled.

In a perfect world, the conversation would end there.

"I want to know if this dress looks sexy," she continued.

If that question where on the SAT, I wouldn't have made it into college.

"Of course it's sexy," I said.

"Why? What part is sexy?"

That was a trick question. I motioned toward the dress. "All of it looks that way."

"Oh you're a big help."

"What? What did I say?"

"Just go back to your TV."

Like I could. "Go back to your TV" is the ultimate multiple-choice test that must be answered very carefully. Here are the choices: A. Go back to TV and suffer. B. Answer the original sexy question wrong and suffer. C. Answer the sexy question right and be accused of being patronizing, which in turn makes you suffer. D. Tell her if she wears that dress in public you'll become insanely jealous, drag her home by the hair, and chain her to the bedroom wall as your sex slave.

For the newlywed who hasn't studied, the correct answer is: D.

"I was thinking of wearing these shoes with them," she stated, placing bright orange heels next to the pine green dress.

"You can't wear those together," I gasped.

"Oh, honey, you *do* care," she cried, wrapping her arms around my neck.

"Of course I do," I said.

She grabbed my hands and placed them on her hips. "Holding me like this, do I feel like I gained weight?"

I broke my number two pencil in half and went back to watching TV.

For all I do for my wife, I ask you, where was she when I had my own weight crisis? When I was faced with moving up a pant size?

She acted as if it weren't a major deal.

But I had been a size 32 way too long to just willy-nilly step up to the 33.

Of course, I understood the ramifications if I didn't make the leap—mainly, before long, my pants would be so tight, I'd lose all sensation in my toes. Experts have told me that when that happened, I'd fall down.

I was wearing a size 30 waist in high school. After college, I stepped up to a size 31, but I wasn't concerned. As I approached the age of 30, my waist expanded to a 32. My worry was if I went to a size 33 now, I'm liable to be in a 34 by the time I'm 40. At that rate, if I lived to be 90, I'd be buried with a tarp around my legs. What would they say at the open casket funeral? "Oh, look Martha, his tie matches the circus tent."

Of course my wife wasn't sympathetic. I told her that I felt fat, and she replied with a five-minute lecture on how women have a lot harder time controlling their weight.

Which is true, and I certainly wouldn't negate their struggles, but that doesn't change the fact that if I didn't hold my gut in, my pant's button might burst off and kill someone.

It's not fair. I haven't dramatically changed my eating habits since my early twenties—in fact, if anything, I eat less. Nonetheless, the weight just seems to be latching onto me like flies on fruit. If I eat one piece of cake, I instantly gain 5 pounds. A steak dinner—6 pounds. Ice cream—4 pounds. Scratch-and-sniff book—1 pound.

It's not like I didn't try to maintain my 32 waistline. I went to the gym, sweated like a pig, ate carrots all day—and still I had to lie on my back and wiggle into my pants like a goldfish out of water. Once, my wife walked in the room while I was getting dressed and thought I was having a heart attack. She started CPR.

What I've discovered, however, is that weight is a relative thing—I blame my grandfather. I can already tell I am in the early stages of inheriting his body. I just hope I don't also get his nickname: Puddin.

As time went on, it became pretty clear that I couldn't avoid the 33s. At first only I noticed, but then, my wife, who, mind you, doesn't feel sorry for me, conceded it was time I stepped up a pants size.

"Go to a size 33? I can't!" I exclaimed.

"Why not?"

"It's a matter of pride," I answered.

She looked me up and down. "Actually honey—it's a matter of seeing the outline of your underwear."

The next day, I bought size 33 waist pants. I put the 34s on layaway.

14

Counting My Blessings

"It's called 'cold cash' because it's never in your pockets long enough to get warm."

—Unknown

The furnace broke down the other day. A week before that, the dryer stopped working. I'm just waiting for the next catastrophe.

My wife, on the other hand, is unfazed.

"Ken, things break—that's a fact of life," she told me. "Stop worrying about it."

Her philosophy that everything will work out is in direct conflict with my vision of shivering outside in a bread line.

"How can you be so calm?" I asked. "I just wrote a $300 check for the dryer, and now the furnace is busted. It's winter—we need heat."

"I guess we'll just have to live a simpler life," she replied calmly.

"How?" I asked. "By wearing a sweater and ski pants to bed?"

She looked up toward the heavens. "I meant we might have

to go without our morning latté break until we've paid off the furnace."

"What are you talking about?!" I shouted. "We might have to go without dinners."

She patted the couch and motioned me to sit down next to her. "Ken, you're overreacting, AGAIN," she exclaimed. "Everything will be fine. You know what you need to do?"

"Open a lemonade stand? Get a paper route?"

"No, you need to count your blessings," she said. "You should write down the things you are thankful for, instead of focusing on what you can't afford."

"You want me to write down all the positive things about being broke?"

She nodded.

So I did. Despite the fact that the furnace doesn't work, I owe $650 to fix it, and payday is several weeks away, the bright side is . . .

- Top Ramen is only 25¢ a pack.

- There is usually loose change under my car seat, behind the couch, or in my daughter's penny loafers.

- I can always rotate a lightbulb from room to room.

- A toothpaste tube isn't scraped clean until it's flayed like a trout.

- There are many emergency alternatives to no toilet paper . . . paper towels . . . napkins . . . coffee filters.

- No one knows my underwear has holes in them. (Reminder: Or wants to know!)

- Little kids think eating popcorn for dinner is fun.

- My New Year's resolution was to lose weight.

- It feels good to know my survival skills are up to par.

- If we are out of sandwich bags, I can always tell my kids it's *Little House on the Prairie* Day at School and put their lunch in a bucket.

- I don't have to pay for my video rental . . . until I return it.

- I can memorize useful excuses in case I am in a pinch. My favorites are: "Oops, I forgot my credit card." Or, "I'll pay next time." Or, "I'm sorry, was this your beer?"

- I could always start a new entertainment trend called "In Bed by Nine."

- Folgers is better than Starbucks . . . I can keep telling myself.

When you are single, you might or might not have a lot of money, but you certainly have 100 percent control over what you do have. This changes to 20 percent control when you get married and to 1 percent if you have kids.

Then, suddenly it's the holidays, and maybe you find yourself sitting around thinking what I was thinking last December: *Had we kept our New Year's resolution, my wife and I would have had enough money saved to buy our kids, ourselves, all the relatives, and the cat nice presents for Christmas, plus have plenty leftover to vacation for a week in Hawaii and keep our kids in new underwear for another year.*

It sounded like a good idea last January when we promised to sock away monthly savings into a special bank account earmarked for the Christmas season. It was an easy decision to make.

The hard part was arriving at December 1 and finding my wife and I staring at our empty savings account like two helpless ants who look both ways on the freeway, don't see any cars, and start to cross.

"Didn't we save any money?!" I yelled.

My wife's eyes rolled. "After school fund-raisers, baby-sitters, and take-out, there wasn't anything left."

To afford Christmas, therefore, my wife and I have had to get industrious. We raked the neighbors' leaves, baby-sat pets, and put a wad of gum at the end of a stick and fished out pennies from the storm drain. We even tried sales, but unfortunately, no one buys lemonade alongside the road from two desperate-looking grown-ups sitting at their daughter's Precious Moments card table.

We did, however, manage to scrape together enough cash for the kids' gifts with a little left over for the relatives. With this in mind, our goal was to buy presents that didn't look as cheap as they cost or could be taken back to confirm their poor taste.

Still, my wife had second thoughts.

"I don't know," she said after we went shopping. "These things for our parents seem awfully cheap."

"Explain that to the kids when they discover we took their piggy banks hostage."

"How are we going to pass these candles off as costing more than $5?" she continued.

"My mom loves candles. They'll be fine."

"She loves ones shaped like cactus?"

"We'll say the children made them," I explained.

"Do you suppose we could tell your brother the kids also made the $5 aftershave we bought him?"

"Yeah, we could pour it into a Mason jar."

"Can't we at least add a little more to these gifts?" my wife asked.

"Good idea," I agreed. "I think the kids have Halloween candy left."

She shook her head. "They licked all of it."

"Not since last week."

"They're all sticky, Ken!"

"Okay, forget the candy. Why don't we sing Christmas carols to the family instead?"

"With your voice?" she exclaimed. "Never mind. Hopefully they'll understand."

"Hopefully they won't buy us nicer presents than we are giving them."

"That's it," my wife cried. "Starting in January, we are saving a little each month for next Christmas!"

"Okay dear, whatever you say," I answered.

I already told the kids to get another year out of their underwear.

Of course, that story probably doesn't surprise you if you caught the *A&E* documentary they recently did on my life. For those who missed it, it went something like this:

Hello and welcome to suburbia. Isn't it a beautiful day? The sky is blue, the daisies are in bloom, and the sounds of automatic sprinklers fill the air.

All is well.

Now, let's take our cameras a little closer, shall we? Here is homeowner and regular family man Ken Swarner. You might not notice it by looking at him, but every time something breaks in his wife's car, Ken doesn't know how to fix it.

Two weeks ago, the window washer fluid ran out. Then, the button to roll down the left back window stopped working. And once, for no apparent reason, the drink cup holder flew off the dashboard and gave his wife's thigh a Charlie horse.

Growing up, Ken never learned to fix a car—that's why Ken's wife is scanning through the phone book, searching for an auto repair shop.

It looks like Ken's thinking, That's going to cost a pretty penny.

Now, notice our suburban male doing what males of his species do when they learn that their wives want to take the car into an expensive shop to be repaired . . . he's trying to fix it himself.

Here he is, sitting in the front seat of the car, staring at the owner's manual like a kindergartner pretending to read. Why is he picking up that screwdriver? Can you superglue a drink cup holder to the dash?

(Episode Two)

Last time, we left our suburban homeowner in his garage . . . quite perplexed. He's now been tinkering on that car for the past three days. He's taking home car repairs very seriously, isn't he?

Gosh, is he really inviting his wife into the garage to see his progress? See him showing her the wires under the dashboard? She has absolutely no idea he just shocked himself, does she? Look at him paste his hair back down with spit.

What's this? He's handing her the keys? What a proud smile he has on his face. Don't worry, he'll get the feeling back on his left side in no time.

There she drives away. I don't think she knows her rear window is stuck in the halfway down position. Wait . . . that's a powerful sprinkler the neighbor has . . . now she noticed the window. She's going to need a large towel. Oops, she's turning around . . . run, Ken, run.

Too late.

See Allison, she has something to say: "Face it, you can't fix a car. It's embarrassing. I think the girls in the carpool are planning to pass around a hat. I guess I can't blame them after they had to shimmy over my front seat because the back doors wouldn't open yesterday. Which wouldn't have been so bad if Kate Crenshaw hadn't grabbed the drink cup holder to balance herself. It snapped completely off—her head left a dent in the dashboard. How are you going to fix that?"

(Episode Three)

Last time we left our suburban homeowner, his wife was shaking her wet hair all over him. It's difficult to determine who is dumber—Ken, for requesting one last chance to fix the car, or his wife, for granting it. We'd ask them right now, but they seem to have their hands full with being stranded on the shoulder of the freeway.

Uh, oh, look out Ken, here comes the inevitable: "I told you so!"

Ouch!

Yep, it's another beautiful day . . .

Whether it's true or not, I think men feel if they turn their backs long enough, they'll wind up out of money and homeless. I admit this is irrational—but it doesn't mean I'm going to stop. That's why my wife walked up to me in July holding a stamped envelope.

"Honey, what's this?" she asked.

"Um, uh, that came in the mail for you," I answered.

"Why was it in the burn barrel?"

"Uh, oh, I must have accidentally dropped it in there when your son ran over my foot with the wheelbarrow."

"It's an invitation to Jennifer's candle party."

"Really?"

"You sound surprised. It seems odd that the invitation has been steamed open," she said, brushing the grass clippings off the flap.

"It's just a shame you missed the party," I exclaimed walking out of the room.

"No I haven't."

My head spun around. "What?! The party was Saturday!"

"Didn't read it, huh? I'll be home at 6."

"Wait!" I yelled as she disappeared into the garage. "How much are you going to spend?"

She shrugged.

"I'm thinking $10," I ventured.

"Thirty dollars," she replied.

"But not a single penny more. Right?"

"Bye."

I ran down the street shouting into her car window. "Just remember, we already have 23 unused rubber stamps in the heating duct, 17 Tupperware containers with 16 missing lids, 2 breadbaskets we never use, and a drawer full of makeup that makes your skin break out—all from those other parties Jennifer gave, so $20, that's all, right? Right? Okay? Okay?!"

After a mile I collapsed. Struggling home, I paced until she returned.

"Hi," I said opening her car door like a valet. "How was the party? Okay, how much did you spend?"

"Let me show you inside where we can spread out." She went to the dining room table and produced two beige candles the size of plums.

I sighed with relief. "I can't believe it, you stayed under budget."

"Almost," she answered proudly.

I froze. "How much?"

"$42.40."

"$42.40—the wax in my ears must be worth a friggin fortune! I thought you said you'd only spend $10."

"I said $30, which you know perfectly well is an estimate."

"Why do you have to buy anything? Can't you just eat the free food and leave?"

She rolled her eyes. "I can't offend Jennifer. You have to buy something."

"Weren't there used candles?"

She ignored me and arranged the two wax remnants on the mantel. "Jennifer's husband is throwing a party."

"Glen?"

"It's a tool party. You should do one, too."

"Oh great, I could soft-sell needle-nosed pliers for two hundred bucks. How could I do that to my friends?"

She looked at me for a long time. "Did you know the person throwing the party gets merchandise for free?"

I wonder if they make invitations shaped like a wrench?

15

Who Volunteered Me?

"Beareth all things, believeth all things, hopeth all things, endureth all things. Charity never faileth."

—I Corinthians, 13:7–8

Good news! Joan Thompson's husband was transferred out of the country. Our PTA chapter can now rest easy again.

Don't get me wrong, I didn't have anything against Joan as a person. In fact, she is one of the nicest people you will ever meet (and she'd do anything for you). But, as president of the PTA, I knew the very fabric of our existence would fray before our eyes as long as Joan Thompson was a member.

Joan is one of those Super Moms (talented, put-together, on time, friendly), and it was hurting the self-esteem of my executive board.

I'll never forget our first meeting at the start of the school year. Joan brought homemade chocolate-and-macadamia-nut cookies topped with yellow school buses made from caramelized sugar. Doris Greenburg, my vice president, brought Chips Ahoy. After the treasurer's report, Doris accidentally broke Joan's school buses with her clipboard.

It went downhill from there.

Our first major project of the year was the school Harvest Carnival. While most of us brought a few white sheets (mine had Charlie Brown on them) and clumps of hay to spread around the room, Joan handpainted large, fanciful leaves the size of satellite dishes to hang from the ceilings. We set up a few activity games around the gym—Joan mapped out a cake-walk and baked twenty cakes of different sizes, shapes, and decoration. We brought juice. Joan simmered hot, spiced apple cider.

I convened an emergency meeting behind the ring toss: "Does anyone else feel like hanging themselves from Joan's leaves?"

Everyone looked close to tears.

"I work," Doris explained. "My son is on a competitive swim team. I can't keep up with this woman. This isn't fair."

Everyone nodded.

"It wouldn't be so bad if she was mean," Patsy added. "But she's so perfect."

"Alright, so who is going to tell her she's out of the PTA?" I asked.

"On what grounds?"

"Making me feel inadequate!"

The carnival came and went. Our next project was a bake sale, and Joan was still a member.

Several tables were stacked with baked goodies. The store-bought crowd transferred their cookies and cakes from the plastic wrap and put them on plates from home. The bake-at-home group put their Duncan Hines and Pillsbury creations next to the others. This left an entire table for Joan's master-pieces—made-from-scratch tortes and confections that rivaled a cruise ship's midnight buffet.

"I think I'm going to throw up," Doris exclaimed.

"Because Joan's cakes are so beautiful?" I asked.

"No," she replied, "because I just ate a piece of what you brought."

The sale was a success, thanks to Joan . . . of course.

Then, luckily, right after Christmas break, Joan's husband was transferred to London. It's not that anyone celebrated publicly or anything. In fact, everyone said they felt bad she was gone. It's just that the members had a hard time feeling awful without cracking a smile.

Now, everything is back to normal. Of course, we have serious doubts we'll make any money at our next craft show without Joan, but at least our pride is back intact.

One of those things they never taught in high school health class about having children is that you instantly become a fund-raising machine.

You don't really think about those things as a kid. I remember when I was ten and my soccer team sold candy bars to raise money for new uniforms. Each player was handed a box of twenty and told to unload them.

My parents bought two candy bars with the understanding that I would canvass the neighborhood for eighteen other charitable souls who saw the value in getting fat so I could look dapper on the soccer field.

At the dinner table each evening, my father asked how the sales were going.

"Great," I'd say. "Sold another one this afternoon."

I told this lie for eighteen days. In truth, I ate all those candy bars, including the two my parents paid for. So when it came time to turn in the money, my teammates had new soccer uniforms to wear while my mom covered my fanny with a wooden spoon.

Twenty-one years ago I might have not been much of a salesman, but after years as a school parent, I have had more than opportunity to redeem myself.

It all began when my son was set to start kindergarten. I asked my neighbor about school supplies and she told me to forget pens and pencils and instead put my money in blank receipt books and copies of our state's sales tax charts. I asked her why and she told me to "brace" myself.

On the first day of school, her comments were clarified when the PTA sent a note home pinned to the new sweater my son ripped at recess. The letter read: "Dear Parents. Our first fund-raiser of the year is selling candles. We are asking each family to sell four so we can afford to replace the Big Toy Mrs. Derkin's class accidentally burned down during their magnifying glass unit."

"Notice," my neighbor explained when I showed her the note, "it said *first* fund-raiser."

"How many will there be?"

"Let me put it this way," she said. "When my grandma came to visit last spring, she had the words 'No Soliciting' scribbled across her forehead with an eyebrow pencil."

Sure enough, last school year my son had something to sell every month, including Christmas and spring break.

On the fifth fund-raiser, sometime in January, I called my mom to see how many pizza coupon books she wanted to buy. The operator said her phone was disconnected and she hadn't left a forwarding message.

So I called my brother. "What happened to Mom?"

"She moved," he said.

"Where?"

"I can't tell you."

"Why?"

"I promised."

"What does that mean?"

"Leave the poor woman alone!" he shouted. "Look, she bought three entertainment books, two tubs of cookie dough, and enough holiday wrap to cover Cincinnati. Your peddling has driven our mom away!" He hung up.

"The cookie dough was for her pinochle group!" I yelled into the dead phone. "They asked her for the recipe! She has no reason to complain!"

Needless to say, my son carried on the rest of his sales year without his grandma.

By the end of the school year, however, my mom returned. She had moved to Tucson, but came back after an industrious summer school there had chartered a bus and blanketed her neighborhood with elementary school kids selling Christmas cards.

I stopped by her house soon after for coffee and reminded her of the time I ate all the candy bars I was supposed to sell for soccer and how mad she and Dad were when they found out. We had a good laugh. That is, until I handed her my son's swim-a-thon sponsorship form.

Boy, I forgot how bad that wooden spoon hurts!

Needless to say, my son finished that school year with $485 in fund-raising sales and 17 relatives who no longer returned our calls. You can imagine how relieved everyone was when summer break arrived.

But, much to our horror, when school started the next fall, the fund-raising machine grew a whole lot bigger. It continues to grow.

Recently, my kids have become popcorn vendors. I just so happened to be volunteering in my daughter's classroom the day a representative from the popcorn company was in town to prepare his sales force.

It began by assembling the students in the gymnasium. Then, to properly hype them into dedicated professionals, the popcorn man used sophisticated motivational techniques—prizes.

He started the sales summit by pulling games and toys out of a bag as if he were Santa on the Home Shopping Network.

"For selling 3,000 cans of popcorn, you can win a trip to Disneyland," he announced.

The kindergartners all wet their pants they were so excited.

My son came running up to me after the assembly. "Dad, if I sell 500 cans of popcorn, I can win a handheld video game!"

I looked at him. "Son, if you sell that much, I'm taking you out of school and opening up a car dealership."

"Cool!"

"Of course," I continued, "you could just tell those who are still taking our phone calls that they don't have to buy the popcorn as long as they give you 10 percent of its price. You could take that money and buy your entire class video games."

The popcorn rep heard me say this and called me a socialist under his breath.

"I'm not one of those!" I yelled after him. "A socialist's family doesn't get unlisted phone numbers."

Of course, my kids love the prizes. They'll huddle around the kitchen table and talk excitedly about which ones they hope to win. Because they are excited, you'd think they'd actually sell some of the product, wouldn't you?

Nope.

But, because my wife and I don't want to look like unsupportive PTA parents, we pick up the slack and sell the stuff to co-workers.

There are some sales, however, that I'm not willing to make. My wife has a difficult time understanding this.

"Why can't you sell to Phil Johnson?" she once asked me.

"He has three daughters in gymnastics," I answered.

"So?"

"Competitive gymnastics."

"And?"

"And," I continued, "if we sell him stuff, we'll have to buy his gymnastic fund-raisers."

"How bad could that be?"

"Do you know what Olympic training goes for these days?"

She shook her head.

"Just one of his daughter's fund-raisers would require a monthly payment plan. Imagine all three."

"What if they made the Olympic team?" my wife said. "Isn't that worth supporting?"

"Sure, we could tell our friends we paid for their training— what a warm feeling that would be as we slept in our refrigerator boxes under the overpass."

Fortunately, we wrapped up our popcorn sales. As usual, my wife and I purchased most of it. We weren't going to buy any this time, but my son sold five cans while my daughter only sold two. So, to even it out at five apiece, we'll be eating popcorn for dinner the rest of this year. For all our efforts, my kids each received a sticker from the prizeman. That's two $100 stickers I'm writing off my income taxes—if the IRS needs more money, I figure they can hold their own fund-raiser!

If it's not money I'm giving, then it's my time—like when I signed up . . . I mean, when my wife signed me up, to be a Cub Scout leader. I agreed to do it thinking that meant hikes, whittling, and survival training.

My assumption would be true, if you're a Boy Scout. Cub Scouts, on the other hand, involves cutting, pasting, and telling the kids to stop painting the backs of their chairs.

The problem here, of course, is that I am artistically challenged. On my first day with my wolf den, I grabbed an armful of red string, glued it to a poster board, and showed it to the kids.

"What is it Mr. Swarner?"

"A valentine for your mom," I answered proudly.

"It looks like spaghetti."

Frankly, I am in uncharted waters. Nothing since kindergarten has prepared me for Cub Scout leadership. In fact, I flunked collage in the first grade.

My wife won't help.

"They're eight-year-olds, Ken. What is so difficult about this?"

"Sock puppets," I explained. "The panda bears we made tonight look like they have eczema."

So to survive, I attended the Cub Scout District Conference to learn more about running my den programs. Let me set the scene: There were more than a thousand grown men in brown shirts and khaki pants holding hands in large circles singing "Found a Peanut." Afterward, we divided into small groups around tables heaped with arts and crafts materials.

"Each craft you make is a testament to your abilities," our table leader explained.

Excited, I grabbed an empty toilet paper roll, laced my belt through it, and called it a belt buckle. I was given the official Cub Scout Arts and Crafts Book and sent home.

Determined not to fail, I took a week off work and studied the book. I made pencil holders out of soup cans for the neighbors. I collected leaves in the backyard and pressed them in books for future generations to enjoy. I even made my wife a macaroni necklace, but it broke on the way to the country club for lobster night. Later, I noticed our dinner guest lean over and tell my wife she had a piece of yarn wedged between her teeth.

Nonetheless, by the time our weekly den meeting rolled around, I felt at one with my craftiness. Afterward, I asked my son how he thought the meeting went.

"Fine."

"I mean, how about the singing, the games, THE CRAFTS?"

"Well, tonight's art project was fun until you told us to cut the paper in half and our snowflakes fell in our juice."

I can't wait until my son is a Boy Scout.

I also can't wait until my daughter is out of Girl Scouts. As cookie chairman of my daughter's troop, it came as quite a shock when my wife told me that the deadline to turn in the unsold cookies had passed.

"What does that mean?" I asked her.

"It means," she replied, "that the thousand boxes of cookies you were sure you could sell at your office and didn't are now yours to buy unless you can unload them next weekend."

"But no one told me there was a cutoff date to return them," I stammered.

"They probably mentioned that at the cookie chairman

meeting that you said you didn't need to attend because there wasn't anything they could teach you since you were top Christmas card salesman in the fourth grade."

I originally volunteered to be cookie chairman because it sounded easy. After all, who can resist a cute little girl selling boxes of Thin Mints and Peanut Butter Patties?

Apparently, a lot of people.

In this day and age of fund-raising overload, even the traditional Girl Scout cookies take some effort to sell. Most people are tired of fund-raisers. So five weeks into the cookie season, and after all the relatives had been contacted, the girls in my daughter's troop were burned out. I was facing the very real possibility that I'd be eating Girl Scout cookies for dinner all summer long.

Therefore, as a last-ditch effort, I worked with the girls all week long, preparing them to be expert saleswomen. We rented Zig Ziegler sales tapes. We watched the Home Shopping Network for tips. I even bribed the girls with my retirement money.

Finally, on the last Saturday of the cookie season, I had all the girls meet me at my house to pick up their boxes before spreading out across town with their mothers.

The girls lined up on my front driveway. For a few moments, I paced back and forth looking into their eyes.

Finally, I asked, "Who are we?"

"Girl Scouts."

"I CAN'T HEAR YOU!"

"GIRL SCOUTS!"

"What's our motto?"

"One hundred percent."

"ONE HUNDRED PERCENT, WHAT?!"

"COOKIES SOLD!"

"Why?"

"To be the best."

"Why else?"

"So Mr. Swarner doesn't have to give the cookies to his family as Christmas gifts."

"So what are we going to do?"

"Sell."

"I CAN'T HEAR YOU!"

"SELL! SELL! SELL!"

"Where are we going to sell them?"

"In front of the grocery stores."

"With what?"

"Our card tables."

"What if the people say no?"

"We'll follow them to their cars."

"What if that doesn't work?"

"We'll lie down on their hoods and cry."

"I CAN'T HEAR YOU!"

"BEG! BEG! BEG!"

I raised my hands into the air. "ALRIGHT, LET'S GET GOING!"

A tear came to my eye as I watched fourteen mini-vans peel out of my neighborhood.

Then, a few hours later, as I was thinking positive thoughts about our sales effort, the mini-vans returned with tired, cranky girls and 600 boxes of Girl Scout cookies.

The next day, as I was looking at the fort my kids built in the garage with the boxes of cookies, I thought to myself, *Good thing I don't sell anything for a living*. Then, I went inside to open a box of cookies for dinner.

———

Then there are organizations like Rotary that often run in conflict with "family time"—like last Easter.

At my weekly Rotary meeting in April, the president of the club made a passionate speech regarding our annual Easter Pancake Breakfast fund-raiser.

"I am calling on ALL members of this club to be at the hall by 6 A.M. to serve hotcakes," he stated.

The membership nodded in agreement—which wasn't surprising, as the average age in the room was sixty.

I imagine I was the only one sitting there choking on my pot roast, wondering how I'd tell my kids they would have to wait until the afternoon to hunt for their eggs because Daddy had to serve pancakes for charity.

After the meeting, I sheepishly walked up to the podium. "President Ted," I said. "I'm not sure I can make the breakfast. I have little kids who . . ."

"Can't make it?" he said loudly. A couple other members turned to listen. "This is our club's biggest fund-raiser—it's important."

The others nodded like a church choir.

"I-I-I . . ." chickened out. I acquiesced under the pressure and left the meeting.

That evening at the dinner table, I decided to carefully prepare my family. So I casually dropped the first hint.

"The big Easter Pancake Breakfast is coming up," I said joyfully.

"More meat loaf?" my wife asked, passing me the platter.

"Everyone has to work at it this year," I continued, flinching in anticipation.

My wife stopped and looked blankly at me.

"Y-y-yeah, and I-I-I was thinking," I continued, "that maybe you and the kids would like to serve pancakes with me."

"What about the Easter egg hunt?" my wife said matter-of-factly.

The kids nodded.

I cleared my throat. "We could do that after the breakfast."

The kids started to cry.

I gulped. "There is a lot of pressure for everyone to work at the breakfast this year," I said quickly. "I have to go."

"Honey," my wife said, her voice cracking. "Are you trying to say that you are canceling Easter?"

"No!" I said reassuringly. "I have it all figured out. We just need to get up earlier this year to hunt for eggs."

"How early?"

"Would 4 A.M. work?"

She flinched. "Why don't we just leave a note telling the Easter Bunny to hide the eggs in the car?" she said sarcastically.

"How will we reach the eggs if we are in our seat belts?" my son asked.

"That's what makes it challenging," she said. "Years from now, you can tell your own kids how much fun it was finding your Easter eggs in a drink cup holder."

I blanched.

"What about church?" she continued. "Or are we taking communion out of a coffee tumbler?"

"No," I said. "We will all silently pray while we serve breakfast."

"Pray the dog doesn't eat the kids' Easter baskets while we're gone?" my wife asked. "Or that syrup doesn't get all over the kid's new Easter outfits?"

"They don't have to dress up."

My wife's face sank. "I spent twenty-three hours making your daughter's Easter dress—while you are destroying our holiday memories, do you mind if I at least have the small joy of seeing my sobbing children properly dressed while serving hotcakes?"

"Okay," I said. "She can wear a garbage bag over the dress."

"I'm going to PRAY I didn't hear that," my daughter chimed in.

"Well, what do you want me to do?" I exclaimed.

"Besides quit Rotary?" she asked.

Of course, I stopped feeling quite so bad about my own volunteering nightmares after I came across this story. I can only imagine what it's like to volunteer as a coach in this community:

> *(Headline)* T-ball walkout prompts season delay
>
> (Jefferson Field—AB) Talks between Maintown Kindergarten T-ballers and coaches broke down Sunday over several unresolved issues, creating the longest player walkout in history.
>
> A nine-day cooling-off period was instated Monday by league commissioners as representatives from both sides returned home to consult with their constituents.
>
> T-ball games have been canceled since June 22, and some parents feel helplessly caught in the middle.
>
> "My son's baseball career is hanging in the balance here," explained Lou Sinclair, father of Maintown first baseman Johnny Ball Hog. "Let's get the politics out of the game and play ball."
>
> A key issue still on the bargaining table includes field

sitting-down time, hats that are too big, and snacks, according to siblings who asked not to be identified.

"I'm not motivated by snacks. This isn't about snacks," said Linda "Dandelion Picker" Johnson. "It's just that snacks equal respect. If some teams are getting candy bars and I'm given a Fig Newton, then there's a lack of respect."

The number one unresolved issue for the players' union is full disclosure of the final score.

Billy "I'm Tired" Lewis says he's been manipulated. "Don't tell me it was a tie or that no one keeps score. I don't buy it. They know who won. So tell us!"

Last week, a strike vote was delayed when coaches agreed to suspend trades for three years. Players argued that since everyone has a 1,000 batting average, what's the point.

The issue of cheering was also resolved.

"The kids didn't want to say 'Two, four, six, eight, who do we appreciate?'" explained Coach Charles Harding. "They said it was 'lame.'"

The players, in good faith, also dropped two arguments last week. They were a health plan for chronic shoulder pain stemming from multiple swipes into the tee, and an elimination of outfield positions since no one hits it past the bases.

An opinion poll released Monday showed public sentiment drawn down the middle.

"In my day, we didn't have all these lawyer dads trying to coach ball," said Ira Greenberg of Mainville. "Our coaches came from the steel mills—they knew what T-ball was all about."

Others blame the players for the impasse.

"I'd like to put them all in time-out," said Vera Jackson

of Maintown. "If this was my kid, he'd be on restriction until he was 18."

League organizers said if a compromise isn't met soon, T-ball will be canceled for the season to make room for fall soccer leagues.

Finally, a quiz:

Question: How many PTA members does it take to screw in a lightbulb?

Answer: Twenty-one. One to screw it in and feel unappreciated, and twenty to stand around feeling slighted because they weren't asked to do it.

16

Calgon, Take Me Away!

> "Bear began to sigh, and then found he couldn't
> because he was so tightly stuck;
> and a tear rolled down his eye, as he said:
> 'Then, would you read a Sustaining Book,
> such as would help and comfort
> a Wedged Bear in Great Tightness?'"
>
> —A. A. Milne

I believe that in the next two decades, we will see the further mainstreaming of New Age thoughts and practices into everyday life. No longer will meditation gurus be labeled whackos, but instead, our children will take those classes between biology and algebra.

Unfortunately, thus far, all the New Age and self-help books I've ever read about reducing stress and living a healthy lifestyle boil down to the same unsaid conclusion: If you're a parent, you're on your own!

Deepak Chopra, in his book *Seven Spiritual Laws of Success,* says, "to gain energy, today I will accept people, situations, circumstances and events as they occur."

Let me get this straight. When my daughter took her Hula Barbie to show-and-tell and she was asked what she liked about it, I should "accept" that she ripped the doll's bikini top off, pointed to its breasts, and said, "I like these."

Stephen Covey, in 7 *Habits of Highly Successful People,* says, "seek first to understand then to be understood."

I tried that. I asked my little girl why she exposed her doll in front of twenty giggling kindergartners, and she said, "I don't know." It was all so much more clear. Then it was my turn to be understood.

Jake Steinfeld, in *You Can Do It* says, "find a go-to person to help provide moral support."

That doesn't work either. I WENT TO my wife to take care of the strip-tease artist, but she locked herself in the bedroom and refused to come out until the kids graduate.

Richard Carlson, in his book *Don't Sweat the Small Stuff,* says, "It's all small stuff."

Believe me, when an elementary school principal calls you at home about a naked doll, she isn't thrilled to hear that advice.

Finally, Louise Hay, in her book *You Can Heal Yourself,* says, "start to listen to what your inner-self is telling you."

My inner voice says, "Spank the child."

Possibly my favorite advice, though, which all the self-help gurus recommend, is to spend 30 minutes a day in quiet meditation or yoga.

Yeah, right!

"Kids, Daddy is meditating right now. Please take the boomerang outside."

"What's meditating?" they asked.

"It's sitting still in a dark room thinking of nothing—just being."

"Is that what Mom's doing? When is she coming out of the bedroom?"

"Look," I said raising my inner voice. "You kids need to be quiet!"

"We want to see you meditate. Are you doing it?" they asked, lifting my closed eyelid.

"I'm trying."

"Does it hurt?"

"No."

"Are you thinking of nothing now?"

"Okay," I moaned. "If you kids will go outside and play for 30 minutes, I'll buy you both an ice cream."

They happily agreed and left.

I closed my eyes and slipped back into my trance.

Two minutes later my daughter came in shouting: "Dad! Alasdair fell down!"

"That's okay," I chant. I was centered. I was at one with my space. I was just being.

"And blood is coming out of his nose on your car!"

If you are really serious about reducing stress, I'd suggest grabbing a New Age book by one of the above authors and RIPPING out all the pages . . . you'll feel better. I did!

Like I said, this movement of granola-eating, Birkenstock-wearing, yoga-loving people have worked their way into modern society and have begun to influence the very foundation of my existence—namely, my wife.

She knew the kids and I wouldn't understand, but she claims she had to do it anyway.

"Ken, kids, I went to a health food store today," she recently announced. "We're changing our diet."

"Oh," I said, scanning the dinner table. There was a plate of steaming chicken, which I recognized, but the salad and two other bowls were definitely holding plant life I couldn't identify. "I thought maybe you went fishing in a pond this morning."

The kids looked frightened.

"Well, you all know I've been reading that book about the health benefits of organic, natural foods," she continued. "So I got up the nerve and bought some new kinds of produce that the book recommended for optimal health."

"What's this?" my son asked, poking at what looked like a giant dish scrubby.

"Kale."

"Huh?"

"It's a vegetable," she explained. "It belongs to the cabbage family."

He blinked. "Maybe we should give it back to them."

My wife smiled. "My book said kale is packed with important minerals."

"So are rocks."

"Is this bamboo?" I said, pulling a yellow slab of something from the salad.

"Yes, that's also an excellent source of vitamins."

"It's a tree."

"I told you I bought a lot of new things."

"Like what else?" I demanded. "Shrubs? Heather? Maybe a hedge for dessert?"

Ignoring me, she picked up the other bowl. "I'm really excited about this," she announced, waving her hand across the soggy, green leaves like Vanna White pretending to be the Farmer in the Dell.

"What is it?" I inquired sheepishly.

"Seaweed."

"Smells really interesting," my son said.

"You think it smells good?" I asked.

"Sure, if you plug your nose like this," he said demonstrating, "and don't breathe in through your mouth."

We passed the serving dishes around the table spooning the vegetables onto our plates.

"The best part about eating this way," my wife said in between bites, "is that everything is 100 percent organic. They don't use harmful pesticides and bug sprays."

"Does that mean there's bugs in it?" my daughter asked.

My wife nodded. "The lady at the health food store did say to check the produce carefully, but I didn't find one creepy-crawly in the bunch. That sold me even more on eating organic."

I smiled and told my wife I appreciated her concern for our health.

She said that the book had given her a newfound mission in life to make us all healthy, and I began to see a certain appreciation for this building around our little table of four, until my son leaned over and said there was something green wiggling between my front teeth.

I pointed to the front of my face. "Honey, is this organic, too?"

My daughter jumped up and ran toward the garage.

"Where are you going?" I shouted as I jammed a butter knife between the gap in my teeth.

"To get a jar with a few holes in the lid," she shouted back. "I want to keep it."

"Great," I exclaimed. "I'll just sit here petting what's left of it until you get back."

Thanks to my wife, eating is now much more of an adventure.

That doesn't hold a candle to when I walked into my bathroom one morning and found her soaking in the tub.

"What's that smell?" I asked.

"My aromatherapy bath salt," she answered. "It's supposed to calm my thoughts and cleanse the toxins out of my body."

"What toxins?"

"Our children, mostly," she exclaimed.

"I thought it was Calgon, take me away? Not," I said, reading her bottle, "essence of lavender and bergamot. Bergamot? What is that, an iceberg about to go off?"

"It's a citrus tree," she answered.

"You're soaking in orange juice?"

"No," she replied, handing me a different packet. "I put some of this frankincense and myrrh in the water. My aura needed a little refreshing."

"Frankincense and myrrh?" I repeated. "You mean the presents the Three Kings gave to Christ? You're soaking your naked body in Jesus' birthday gifts?"

She nodded.

"My God," I exclaimed, "why don't you just go to church and bathe in the holy water?"

"Huh?"

"Sure, you could tell the priest: 'I hope you don't mind me washing in the baptismal font, Father, but I am trying new ways to get in touch with my inner self. Oh, and by the way, when you have a moment, could you please bless my bottle of bergamot?'"

She rolled her eyes. "I think you would be surprised, Ken, how relaxing this is. Aromatherapy is especially uplifting. You've been complaining how stressful work and the kids have been; maybe you shouldn't knock it until you've tried it."

I left the room laughing. In all honesty, I couldn't get the whole business out of my mind. I started wondering if, in fact, a warm, aromatherapy bath might not be the answer to the stress and toil of my life. Finally, when my wife was out look-ing at new homes with our Realtor, I grabbed her essential oils and headed for the bath.

It felt great. The aroma was intoxicating. The fragrance lit-erally took away the tightness in my shoulders and the stress around my temples like magic. My wife was right, it felt great. Gosh, I was so relaxed, I almost didn't notice the real estate agent nosing around in our linen closet.

"Hi," I said waving my loofah sponge.

"Oh!" she exclaimed, glancing suspiciously at my bergamot as she rushed nervously out of the bathroom.

Come to think of it, she looked like she could have used a little Frankincense and myrrh herself.

17

Jingle Bells, Batman Smells

"Party-spirit, which at best is but the madness of many for the gain of a few."

—Alexander Pope

The holidays are a joyous, magical time as the twinkling lights, scrumptious buffets, mystery, and celebration reflect back to us in the smiles of our children. They are also DAMN exhausting!

We go Christmas-tree-hunting at the local U-cut farm each year.

"How about this one?" my wife shouted.

I trudged through the icy mud to where she was standing. Kneeling down, I looked at the massive base of the tree. "Honey, I think we're in the old growth section. Where are the trees you don't need Paul Bunyan to cut?"

"But this one looks good," she argued. "See how the branches are soft and supple, the angles are proportionate, and there isn't a bald spot?"

"Sweetie, you are looking for a tree, not a date. That's too big to cut."

"But it's perfect," she explained.

I looked incredulously at her. "Oh, I see. The tree can't have any defects, but it's okay that I'm in bed all week with a dislocated shoulder?"

I was about to win when she brought out the holiday guilt. "Don't you want the best tree for your kids?"

I looked at my children. Pine needles were stuck to the candy-cane sheen they had all over their faces.

"Fine," I conceded. "But grab my medical insurance card now in case the medi-vac guys need it right away."

An hour later, the mighty tree fell to the earth. And for my two pulled muscles and splitting headache, I paid $40.

Dragging the tree to the car, I stared blankly at my wife.

"What are you waiting for?" she asked.

"A crane to lift the tree onto the roof of the car."

After several attempts to hoist the tree up myself, I heard my daughter's voice: "Where's Daddy?"

"On the ground," my wife answered. "Ken, what are you doing down there?"

"I'm just resting," I replied. "When you guys finish your hot chocolate, I'll probably be ready to roll the tree off my chest."

I finally managed to tie the tree down to the roof, and we drove home. The next challenge was fitting the huge stump into the little tree stand.

"How's it going?" my wife asked, stepping out into the garage where I was trimming the stump with a Skill saw.

"How do you feel about an ornamental tree for the dining room table?" I asked. "I could cut off the top third of this thing and throw away the rest."

"So on Christmas morning we can sit around the table and open gifts?" she asked, sarcastically. "That will be fun. If you put it on your nightstand, we don't even have to get out of bed."

When the tree was finally in the stand, I brought General Sherman into the living room. Kneeling by the stand, I asked my family to help me set it straight.

"How's that look?" I asked, immersed in tree limbs.

"A little to the left," they sang.

"Is that good?"

"To the right."

"There?"

"Left."

"Okay?"

"There—don't move!" my wife shouted. "That's perfect. It's standing straighter than ever before—how'd you do that?"

"By accidentally wedging my hand in the tree stand," I answered. "This is probably going to be awkward during our holiday party next week."

Later that night, after the lights were strung and my wounds were bandaged, my wife and kids decorated the tree.

"Look, Daddy's pretending to be a step stool," my daughter said, standing on me to place an ornament up high on a branch.

"Actually," my wife said. "I think Daddy passed out."

Ow Tannenbaum!

If I'm not cutting down a tree in December, I'm usually at one of the many holiday parties organized by people with too much free time. Unfortunately for me, I'm not much of a conversationalist (hence why I write for a living). Last year I sought professional help.

"I've been worried lately, Doctor. I can't go to a party without experiencing a severe case of anxiety. I stand mute in the corner, clutching my drink as if it's either a life preserver or a sci-fi deflection shield while everyone else floats effortlessly around the room chatting up a storm. Do you know what I mean?"

He nodded. "What are your symptoms?"

"Well, take for instance last weekend. My wife and I were invited to the Johnson's Christmas party. Ten minutes after arriving, I didn't have anyone to talk to so I tested the house plants for moisture."

"Is that it?"

"I wish. So no one would take pity on me, I picked up this month's copy of *National Geographic* and read the story on dust mites as if I hadn't already pored over it at last week's holiday party. Then, to add insult to injury, I walked aimlessly around the room hoping a guest would lean into my space and say, 'Ken, we were just talking about you. What's your opinion on National League teams playing the American League?'

"No one stopped me, so I saddled up to the punch bowl hoping to strike up a conversation through osmosis. Two IVs later, I was relieved to have to go to the bathroom where I whittled away ten enjoyable minutes reading soap labels. When I was done there, I helped the hired staff with the dishes, tightened the bolt on the upstairs shower door, then fixed the vertical hold on the Johnson's TV.

"No one talked to you?"

"One guest asked me to come over the next day and fix his television set. I made $75."

"You didn't try to initiate a conversation?"

"What am I going to talk about? The weather? That's as bright as remarking: 'Oh, I see you're wearing a green shirt today. Your wife said you'd be in blue, but here you are in green. Boy, you just can't predict that stuff.' No, I'd rather pretend to tie my shoelaces twenty times than make a fool of myself. In fact, after I tucked the Johnson's kids into bed and read them a story, I had a few extra minutes to vacuum out my car, so all wasn't a loss."

"What about your wife?"

"There's not a topic of conversation she can't pretend to know something about. She spent a half-hour talking to the Johnson's neighbor while he trimmed his hedge before she even came into the party. She doesn't even know the guy. I think I'm an embarrassment to her though, because later, as I passed by a group, I overheard my beloved lie, 'Ken just had triple root canal, so that's why he looks dizzy this evening.'

"Boy, she's lucky I didn't say anything."

I did say something to my mom last Christmas, however.

Every family has one. A holiday-decoration junkie with a house filled to the brim with knickknacks, crafts, and 12,000 tons of tinsel.

Over the years, my mother has amassed a collection to rival Hallmarks everywhere. So you can understand how absurd this question was.

"Did you notice anything different in the house?" she asked me when I stopped over for a visit.

"Do you mean the seventeen snowglobes on the back of the toilet?"

"Those old things?" she chuckled. "No, I mean here in the living room."

I glanced around the museum. "Well, Dad's missing. Is that it?"

"No," she replied. "This." She pointed to a beaded dollie in the shape of a poinsettia.

I feigned excitement. "Boy, I hope my name's on that in your will."

She smiled from cheek to cheek.

"So where's Dad?" I asked.

"I don't know," she answered. "The last time I saw him he was on the couch."

"The couch with 107 stuffed Santa Clauses?"

She nodded.

"Mom!" I exclaimed.

"What?"

"How do we know Dad's not trapped under there with nothing to eat but peppermint candies?"

She stared at me.

"Isn't this a wake-up call?" I continued. "Where are we all going to sit on Christmas Day?"

"We can all fit in here."

"No we can't. We're going to have to line up our cars in the driveway and pass gifts to each other through the windows. The kids will have to call you on your cell phone to say thank you."

"Now why would you say that?" she answered. "It's not that bad."

"You have eighteen stockings hanging at the fireplace."

"So?"

"So, there are only eleven of us in the family. You're sort of old to be adopting children, aren't you?"

She rolled her eyes.

"Mom, do you even know half of what you have here? Do you buy these things just for the sake of owning them?"

"Now hold it right there!" she exclaimed. "Every one of these decorations are special to me. I bought them for myself whenever something wonderful happened. They remind me of important events."

"Really?"

She walked around the room. "I bought this puffy snow-man after my bridge group won the regional championships. I picked up this candy cane candle when my granddaughter was born. And I got this snowglobe on my thirtieth wedding anniversary."

"And this one?" I asked, holding a pinecone wreath.

"I passed my emission's test."

"This one?"

"I nursed a fern back to life . . . it would want me to have it."

I turned around to leave.

"Where are you going?" she asked.

"To file a missing person's report on Dad," I answered. "And then I'm going to clean out my car for Christmas Day."

And if that's not enough, the following poem will surely put the holidays in perspective:

Sugar Plums

'Twas the night before Christmas, and all through the street
Not a creature was sleeping, my body was beat;
The stockings were taped to the chimney quite snug,
In hopes that my kids wouldn't give them a tug;
My daughter was jumping on top of my bed,
While visions of broken things danced in my head;
And mamma getting ready, and I with a comb,
Were almost prepared to drive to my folks' home,
When somewhere downstairs there arose such a clatter,
I sprang from my room to see what was the matter.
Away to the stairs I flew like an ace,
Tripped over the Legos and fell on my face.

The bruise on my head and my pain swelling side,
Gave a luster of midnight to objects inside,
When, what to my crestfallen eyes should appear,
But my rambunctious son, with a face full of tears,
With a little hors d'oeuvre plate, so empty and bare,
I knew in a moment he dropped it downstairs.
More rapid than squirrels my anger it came,
and I whistled and shouted and called them by name;
"You dropped fruit! Rocky road! The truffles! And sweets!
The tea cakes! The crackers! What will Uncle Dutch eat?!
To the top of the stairs! To the rooms down the hall!
Now sweep it up! Sweep it up! Sweep it up all!"
As mad dogs that before the wild tornado fly,
When they meet with their parent-folk, fit to be tied,
So out to the auto my family we flew,
With an armful of gifts and the damaged treats, too.
And then, in a flurry, we arrived at my folks'
Their puppy was barking, my kids gave it pokes
As I fell in a chair and was spinning around,
Down the hallway my mom and dad came with a bound.
Mom was dressed all in red, from her feet to her yoke,
And her clothes were all blemished with Jell-O and smoke;
A trayful of food she had spilled on her lace,
And she looked like a toddler just feeding her face.
My dad—how he hugged us! His laughing how jolly!
My kids jumped on his back and called him a trolley!
My tight little mouth was drawn up like a bow,
And I shot words off my lips like darts at a foe;
"Children be careful, Papa's back is quite bad!
If he throws a spinal disk, you'll make Grandma mad!"
The plates were set and the dinner was ready
My son gave the prayer that included his teddy,

The room was jammed with people, tables, and chairs,
My nephew threw stuffing into his dad's hairs;
A flash of Gram's eyes and a shake of her head,
Soon gave him to know he had something to dread;
We spoke many words and went straight to our meals,
And ate all the fixings despite how we'd feel,
Then sometime around 12 we expressed our last joys,
And returned back home to assemble the toys.
We placed the last gifts, and I gave a tired yawn,
I made a silent prayer, to sleep hopefully past dawn.
But my son did exclaim, as I walked past his door,
"Happy Christmas dear Dad, I'll wake you 'round 4."

18

Season of Change

"It ain't over till it's over."

—Yogi Berra

My grandmother died this past year at the age of 93, and on that melancholy day, my son asked me what she was like.

"I don't know," I told him, "because she had lived a ways away and I only saw her around Christmastime and the occasional summer."

My answer was less than satisfying for this little boy who lives within a five-mile radius of all four of his grandparents. He thought about it for a little while and then asked: "You mean she never zipped you up when your fly was open?"

Times have changed. We hear constantly that more and more grandparents are taking an active role in their grandchildren's lives. While the majority provide the ultimate traffic control for parents harried from the rat race, in some cases, these senior folks are actually raising their children's children on their own.

I imagine when one of my son's grandmas dies years from

now and he is asked to provide the eulogy, it will go something like this:

"Grandma would be very happy to know that I come before you today in new shoes and my hair combed. How I looked was very important to her. Not because I had to be perfect; she just wanted me and the world to know that I was taken care of. While my parents rushed us kids around from the grocery store to soccer practice to church, Grandma was always running alongside our car reaching inside with a brush and a clean change of clothes.

"Grandmas are like that, aren't they? By the time their grandchildren come hooting and hollering into the world, they have made all the mistakes, climbed all the social ladders, and worried enough about themselves. As if God has given them license to play, they are suddenly at peace and ready to bring joy and happiness to our lives . . . even though we sometimes squirm in their laps, wake up Grandpa, and forget to say 'thank you.'

"There's the old joke about how great it is to be a grandparent because you can spoil the kids and then give them back to their parents. Only, in my case, Grandma usually sent us home with Grandpa so he could fix something in our house, two Tupperware containers filled with leftovers, and the loud, battery-operated toy we always wanted but our parents refused to buy.

"Then there was the time we didn't go home at all—in fact, we lived with Grandma for six months while our house was being built. For 180 days, I discovered what it meant to be a prince . . . though my dad said I acted like the court jester.

"It's an absolutely wonderful feeling to be perfect in someone's eyes. Dad always said 'If she only knew . . .' Well, I think she did, but she didn't care if I failed a test, hit my sister, or didn't clean my room. What did that have to do with anything important?

"There wasn't a week that went by that I didn't see my grandma when I was a kid. We played games, sang songs, laughed, cried, and, most important, shared this world with each other."

And then quietly, pushing back a flood of tears, my son will say "Good-bye, Grandma. Sorry again for breaking your prized bowling trophy."

It's a pity I didn't have this same relationship with my own grandma. I just hope I can be a great grandpa.

I think what's interesting about growing older is how great the past looks . . . especially since I was so eager to grow up during a time that now looks so good.

And even though they say you can't go back, I plan to test that theory. Because this summer is going to be perfect. I'll wake up inside a super-padded Coleman sleeping bag with flannel lining in my backyard to the sound of automatic sprinklers. I'll roll out of the bag in the T-shirt and cutoffs from the day before, which will also suffice for the day ahead, and walk inside just in time for *Starblazers* on the TV.

Wolfing down a bowl of Quisp, I'll rush outside where others my age have congregated for no intended purpose other than to hope something will happen because we have every justification to expect that it will. After a few games of 500 and dodgeball, in which someone's younger brother goes home crying, a mate with acute hearing will hear the melodic chimes of nursery rhymes plinking in the distance. The morning dew will be suddenly shaken off the grass blades by the infamous Calvary call: "ICE-CREAM MAN!"

Like ants rushing to jam, we'll drop our mitts and bats in the middle of the road and bolt for our wheels. Rolling out of our garages and to the edges of our driveways, we'll stare back and forth down the street at each other like geese ready to form that dramatic flying V on a pilgrimage to the Promised Land. Hopping on my bright purple Schwinn with the matching banana seat, I'll give a mighty "follow me guys" as my Keds start turning furiously on top of the two-inch-thick pedals.

Moments later, beyond our heap of bicycles, we'll sit in the largest tree we can find to savor our treats. Of course, someone will accidentally drop their Cap'n Crunch or Push-Up to the ground and be unmercifully razzed the rest of the day—no matter how much he protests that the ice cream was fine once he brushed the blanket of dirt off it.

As the late morning sun begins to bake the ice cream smudges into our pores, we'll hop the fence at the public golf course, peel off our shirts, and roll down the largest grass hill in town. After laying for ten minutes naming the shapes created by the clouds above, we'll walk away, still dizzy, with those nagging grass itches all over our skin that can only be soothed by a quick jump in the water hazard.

After a satisfying lunch of peanut butter and jelly on white bread, chips, and green Kool-Aid, we'll reassemble for the afternoon.

With the sun scorching our unprotected skin, we'll build a huge village in the sandbox, then, ignoring the strict orders not to, we'll crank the hose on full blast and pretend the Hoover Dam has just blown.

Next, someone—probably the guy who's tired of the "you dropped your ice cream" jokes—will grab the hose and start World War III. When something finally breaks, we'll scatter to our homes swearing we had nothing to do with it.

Then it's time for a few lazy moments in the hammock with a glass of ice tinkling inside an elixir of lemonade followed up with back-to-back reruns of the *Brady Bunch*—the afternoon capped off with a boiled hot dog.

Later, when my son walks into my den moaning, "There's nothing to do," I'll wake up from this wonderful day-dream . . . AND TELL HIM TO GO MOW THE LAWN!

Then I'll close my eyes, hoping to rejoin the action just in time for a rousing game of flashlight tag.

Epilogue

It's Worth the Effort

"A question that sometimes drives me hazy: Am I or are the others crazy?"

—Albert Einstein

There's nothing like a new car in the neighborhood to bring the guys together.

"Nice car, Wayne," I said.

Mike crossed over from his house: "Hey Wayne, new or used?"

"Used."

John was two steps behind Mike. "Six or eight cylinders?"

"Four."

Jim peeked over the fence: "CD or cassette?"

"Neither."

We were all impressed. Then, the new neighbor appeared out of nowhere and stole Wayne's moment.

"Wow, look at that!"

We stared, our mouths dropped open, as Bob Henderson parked his new Mercedes in his driveway. We watched him walk inside.

"No kids, you know," Mike said breaking the silence.

"Probably waiting until they've gone through their selfish stage."

"Yeah," we chimed. We had enough kids among us to field our own Little League team—batboy included.

Jim pointed to the Mercedes. "Imagine owning a beautiful car like that with no one kicking the back of your seat."

"Ever notice how baby formula cuts through new car smell faster than a toddler passes salsa?"

"Yeah," we said.

"I saw his wife and him going out again last night. All dressed up."

"Must be nice not paying for a baby-sitter."

"We received a lovely card the other day from our sitter thanking us for the 401(k) and profit-sharing plan."

"He leaves early and comes home late from work any time he wants."

"Wives only want us around for crowd control."

"Yeah," we chanted.

"I bet his watch doesn't get buried in the backyard like treasure."

"I doubt he's ever worked all day oblivious to a Barbie sticker on his butt."

"He can eat his dinner while it's hot."

"And not standing up."

"Yeah," we said, standing there shaking our heads.

Wayne's wife brought out a tray of lemonade. "What are you guys staring at?"

Wayne gestured across the street: "The neighbor's new car. We were just saying if they had kids it . . ."

"They can't have children, you know," she announced.

The five of us looked at each other.

"They're infertile." She passed out the lemonade and returned to the house.

Except for the tinkling of ice against the glasses, it was quiet for a long time.

"It's a nice car, Wayne."

"I think I'll go see what my kids are doing."

"Yeah."